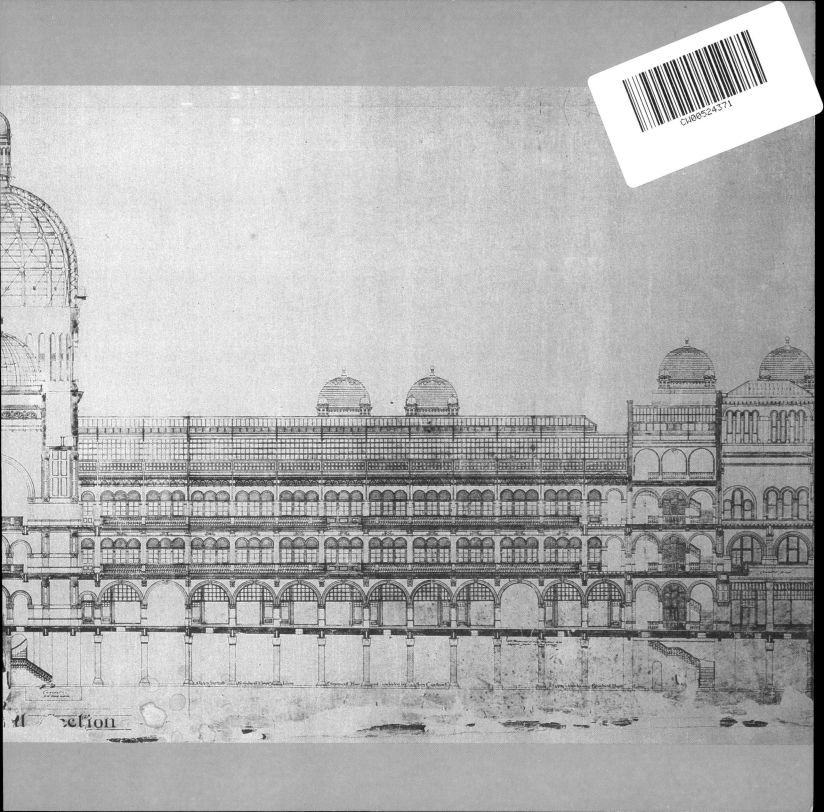

ll   ction

THE QUEEN VICTORIA BUILDING 1898-1986

This book is dedicated to the memory of David Earle, the research architect who contributed so much to the restoration of many of Sydney's historic buildings.

Photograph Council of the City of Sydney.

First published in 1987 by Wellington Lane Press,
1 King George Street, McMahons Point, N.S.W. 2060.

Printed in Singapore by Tien Wah Press.

Typesetting by K-Tek Graphics, 122 Arthur Street, North Sydney, N.S.W. 2060.

Designed by John Witzig.

Artwork by Matthew Neville.

Photo research by Joanna Collard.

Copyright © 1987 John Witzig & Company
P.O. Box 1744, North Sydney, N.S.W. 2060.

National Library of Australia Cataloguing-in-Publication data.

Shaw, John, 1931 (May 10)-
QVB The Queen Victoria Building 1898-1986.

ISBN 0 908022 05 0
ISBN 0 908022 06 9 (pbk.).

1. Queen Victoria Building (Sydney, N.S.W.). 2. Historic buildings — New South Wales — Sydney — Conservation and restoration. 3. Sydney (N.S.W.) — Buildings, structures, etc. I. Title. II. Title: The Queen Victoria Building 1898-1986.

994.41

This book is published as a result of the initiative of Stephenson & Turner Sydney Pty. Ltd., and with the support of the joint venture architects, Rice & Daubney Stephenson & Turner.

THE QUEEN VICTORIA BUILDING 1898-1986

John Shaw

Photograph David Moore.

WELLINGTON LANE PRESS
SYDNEY

The Right Worshipful
THE MAYOR
AND MAYORESS OF SYDNEY
Alderman & Mrs Matthew Harris
request the pleasure of the Company of
The Misses Buckle
at a BALL to be held in the TOWN HALL
on Thursday, 21st July, at 8.30 p.m.
to celebrate the opening of the
QUEEN VICTORIA
MARKET BUILDINGS

Ipoh Garden Berhad

The author wishes to thank the following for their assistance and cooperation during research:
George Kringas, Ross Gardner, Toni Fitzgerald, James Barrett, Robert Trengove, Jennifer Taylor, and
the staffs of the *Sydney Morning Herald* Library, the City of Sydney Public Library, the Mitchell Library,
the State Library of N.S.W., the Archives Office of N.S.W., the Council of the City of Sydney Archives,
the Waverly Public Library and the Royal Australian Historical Society. The thesis on George McRae
by Stephen Booker was also of considerable assistance.

CONTENTS

THE QVB: GASLIGHT TO SATELLITE

WHEN the Queen Victoria Building — a municipal market on the grand scale of a cathedral — was opened in a golden key ceremony on Thursday 21 July 1898, the Mayor of Sydney, Matthew Harris, declared: 'It may be truly said that we have here built for the future as well as the present.'

It was a deceptively simple statement, often forgotten in the following years. At first it seemed little more than the sort of copperplate cliche common enough in civic speeches. In fact, the Mayor's words were both cautionary and prophetic. The City Council had plunged into debt to construct the new municipal market for the century that was about to begin. The city fathers' faith in the future and in the Queen Victoria Building was tempered by expert advice that more than a generation would be needed for the building to acquire financial foundations as solid as its massive granite pillars. Mayor Harris proved to be prescient for an even longer period and the Queen Victoria Building proved indeed that it had been built to last.

After almost a century of changing fortunes, the building retained strength and style enough for a new start and a new role. Its foundations had been laid in the era of gaslight and hansom cabs. Its restoration and rebirth in 1986 as a retailing centre have been reported across the world by satellite.

In 1897 the building was named in honour of Queen Victoria on the occasion of her Diamond Jubilee. The restoration is the most extensive of any major public building of the Victorian era anywhere. An early concept for redevelopment had been initiated in 1976 by the Sydney architects Stephenson & Turner. In 1980 Ipoh Garden Berhad, represented by Mr Yap Lim Sen, assembled the team which went on to bid successfully for the project and the joint venture of Rice & Daubney, Stephenson & Turner was formed to provide the necessary architectural services.

The commercial enterprise inspired by those plans is unprecedented in style and scale. A $75 million investment by Ipoh Garden Berhad has converted an acre of dusty history into a modern shopping centre. The architects have combined and complemented late nineteenth-century elegance and character with late twentieth-century economics and technology.

The distinctive designs of the Queen Victoria Building were and remain both sedate and spectacular — a combination of gallery, arcade and indoor boulevard within Romanesque facades topped by domes and glass roofs covering an entire city block. Unlike the Sydney Opera House, its construction (1893-98) and shape did not provoke controversy. But when completed, the vast building soon fell prey to financial and political troubles. Later, demolition was threatened on several occasions and vigorously resisted. The recurring debates about the building's future — and indeed the question of whether it would have a future at all — were noisy even by the standards of Sydney, a city that has always been vocal about its landmarks.

In summary, the Queen Victoria Building took five years to build, eighty years to diminish and three years to restore to —

Above: The site of the Queen Victoria Building, showing the George Street Markets in 1870. Twenty years before their demolition, the Markets show no sign of being 'miserable' or a 'disgrace' as they were to be later described by aldermanic critics.
Photograph N.S.W. Government Printer.

Left: A beach scene at Sans Souci around the time of the construction of the QVB. The people of Sydney sought relief from the hot summer days on the beach — but fully clothed.
Photograph John Paine: Collection McLeay Museum.

Architect George McRae's perspective of the New
City Markets from York and Market Streets. His
original drawings (still on file in the Sydney Town
Hall) were on fine starch-impregnated linen. The
drawings were made in 'Chinese' or 'Indian' ink
with ruling pens.
Council of the City of Sydney.

The clustered domes of the newly completed Queen Victoria Markets Building, 1898. The majestic main dome was clad with copper sheeting. Its lantern and cupola were fabricated in copper imitating masonry. The twenty lesser domes, made from pressed 'Muntz Metal', simulated stone-tiled Byzantine church domes.

Photograph Mitchell Library.

The finished interior 1898 showing the ground floor
promenade known as the Avenue, the two gallery
levels, and the glazed barrel vault roof.
Photograph Mitchell Library.

The York Street facade of the Building in the early 1900s. The cast iron posted awning was later replaced by a cantilevered awning.

Photograph Mitchell Library.

and beyond — its former glory. The archives show that the QVB was created by a grand municipal gesture, then vandalised by bureaucrats, threatened by political tides, defended by public outcry, reprieved by civic wisdom and finally given new life by private enterprise.

The decades of disputes about its fate embroiled politicians, architects, developers, citizens and conservationists. Eventually their arguments produced democratic agreement commanding wide public and financial support. Exactly 90 years after the City Council had decided to build 'the George Street New Markets' — at a cost of 261,102 pounds 10 shillings and 9 pence — the Council of 1982 decided to lease the landmark for 99 years to Ipoh Garden Berhad for renovation and revival. The decision, said the *Sydney Morning Herald,* would 'restore an important part of Sydney's architectural heritage'.

When this part of the national estate was built in 1893-98 the country was not yet a nation. Federation, which in 1901 united six of Queen Victoria's colonies into the Commonwealth of Australia was still a few years away. The great political warriors of this period of rising Australian nationalism were Alfred Deakin, Edmund Barton and Henry Parkes. Their speeches in the Federation campaigns were being reported and supported by Sydney's leading editor J. F. Archibald, who had founded the *Bulletin* a few years earlier. In the year that construction of the QVB began, *Bulletin* contributors included Henry Lawson, A. B. 'Banjo' Paterson, and Harry 'The Breaker' Morant. Also

active in Sydney at that time were Australia's finest painters, Tom Roberts and Arthur Streeton. The *Bulletin* called Streeton 'the Australian high priest of the impressionist craze' in reviewing his paintings of Sydney's harbour and beaches. In 1894 Sir Henry Parkes reluctantly took time off from politics to sit for a portrait 'for the cause of art and Tom Roberts'.

In Sydney that year, two other artists were in the making: schoolboy batsmen named M. A. Noble and Victor Trumper scored 152 and 67 respectively in their first game for New South Wales. Sydney rode out to the cricket, and to the racecourse at Randwick, which was installing the new-fangled 'starting machines', on steam trams. As they hissed and clanged along George Street, their open top decks gave passengers grandstand views of excavations for the QVB. Often the trams were held up by horse-drawn waggons hauling away endless loads of clay and sandstone. The building was making its first marks on Sydney.

Labourers were paid 5 shillings a day for the pick and shovel work and the jobs were eagerly sought because the city (population: 450,000) was struggling to emerge from recession. The QVB was a tangible symbol of confidence in recovery. After a run on some banks, credit was flowing again and in 1893 the City Council had little difficulty in borrowing 300,000 pounds (the equivalent by some measures of $30 million in the 1980s) to finance its decision to replace the old George Street markets. These ramshackle relics of early Sydney had been patched together between 1831 and 1869 near George Street. By 1888 this warren of stalls, sheds and roofed

The interior of the Singer Sewing Machine shop
showing the elaborate Wunderlich pressed metal tiles
on the walls.

Photograph Singer.

In 1918 the gracious internal spaces began to disappear. Here workmen are installing metal frames to support a leadlight ceiling over the ground floor during the radical 'remodelling' which eliminated the Avenue. The photo shows beams at upper levels carrying new galleries within the widths of the original voids, allowing shopfronts to be brought forward to increase rentable area.

Photograph Milton Kent: Council of the City of Sydney.

alleys selling meat, vegetables and livestock was being described by aldermen as 'miserable' and a 'disgrace to the metropolitan city of the Mother colony'. They could hardly overlook this affront to their civic pride: the dilapidated markets were within sight and smell of the Town Hall with its splendid new concert hall.

However, the Council's reasons for replacing the markets on such a grand scale were not clear. Its motives seemed mixed. In one sense, the QVB was built simply because an inviting central site was available; perhaps, like nature, municipal minds abhor a vacuum. Intercolonial rivalry was another factor. In 1880 Melbourne had opened its towered and domed Exhibition Building. Sydney's response, the steel and glass Garden Palace, burned down in 1882 — 'no one who saw it can the sight forget, nor history cease to pen it with regret', lamented a doggerel of the day.

Apparently the Council, determined to again think and build big, did little market research about demand for retail space in the city centre. Sydney's population had expanded almost tenfold in the previous forty years and, in the confident Victorian vision, growth was taken for granted. But the Council had already built new trading halls on the southern edge of the city and the 'downtown' population was known to be shrinking as new suburbs sprouted along the spreading tram and rail lines. And six private retail arcades, including the fashionable Strand Arcade, had been built in the previous decade.

Nevertheless, the Council hurried ahead in leap-frog fashion. Based only on sketches by City Architect George McRae, excavations began in March 1893, five months before the Council had even decided on the design of what was to rise from the hole as big as two football fields between George and York Streets. During the digging, McRae was frantically drafting. The Council seemed determined to stay one jump ahead of him — invitations for tenders for the steel and iron superstructure were being written when McRae presented the Council with four alternative facades. A professional journal of the day described them as 'scholarly Renaissance', 'picturesque Queen Anne', 'classic Gothic', and 'American Romanesque'. The Council briskly selected the latter, a spectacular addition to Sydney's streetscape and skyline.

Five years later when the magnificent building opened for business, Council policies had produced a monument to civic energy and a chronic economic headache. The councillors proved far better builders than managers. They were advised that competitive rents would repay their investment in thirty years, but they sought quicker returns. The market basement, which the *Bulletin* derided as 'the biggest cabbage shop in town' attracted few produce merchants, despite novel elevators to carry their horses and carts down from street level. High rents also meant that there was no rush for the gallery and arcade shop spaces. The Australian-Chinese Mandarin merchant, Quong Tart, and such prestige clients as Penfold's Wines and the Singer Sewing Machine Company, took leases.

But before long Council was cutting, covering and cluttering

The removal of the original posted awning in June
1918. The Post and Telegraph Office occupied this
position on the corner of York and Druitt Streets
from 1902.

Photograph Council of the City of Sydney.

Opposite: In the 1930s the nineteenth century facade acquired a superb art deco feature when the Sydney County Council — the electrical authority for the city — moved in. During restoration the facade and interior were donated to the Museum of Applied Arts and Sciences.

Photograph Council of the City of Sydney.

Above: In 1959, the then Lord Mayor of Sydney, Alderman Harry Jensen, with a model of a proposal to replace the Queen Victoria Building. Also shown are sketches of other schemes which retain the central dome of the building but add incongruous tower blocks and street facades.

Photograph John Fairfax and Sons.

Scaffolding and hessian shroud the Victorian authority of the building during restoration. W.P. McIntosh's opulent sculptures in Carrara marble were installed above the main entrances in George and York Streets after the opening in 1898. The figures depicted Australia distributing honours to commerce and the arts.

Photograph Jenny Blain.

the stylish interiors in their search for sellable space. The City Library moved in, its readers lulled by the bouquet from Messrs Penfold's products in the basement. It was suggested that the whole place be sold to the new railway system tunnelling its way downtown. In 1916 an alderman offered to buy it. In 1934 the Council moved their offices into the building, and the Electricity Department smothered Victorian surfaces with art deco fittings. Gallery voids were covered over and the gracious glass barrel vaults were sealed. The mutilation continued with the insertion of clerical cubicles, car parking and air raid shelters. Victorian visions vanished under layers of ugly additions.

Oddly enough, the greatest affront to the desecrated building proved to be its salvation. In 1959 Alderman Harry Jensen, supported by several prominent architects, proposed it be demolished to make way for a city square with underground parking. For once Mr Jensen, a popular and competent Mayor, misread the temper of his city. A tug of war over the QVB had been shaping up for some years. An international hotel chain had considered building a 400-room hotel on the site. Another company offered to lease a hotel there if the City Council would build it. A group of Sydney businessmen offered to take a 21-year lease. The Electricity Department (which had become the County Council) was thinking of moving out. There was talk of moving in more civic offices. Alderman Jensen's radical plan had the virtue of stimulating serious debate. Sydney's postwar construction boom had begun and the shape and style of the city was in question.

Suddenly, architecture and the urban environment were public issues. In 1960 architect Robin Boyd published *The Australian Ugliness*, which brought heat as well as light to the debate. In the case of the QVB, the exchange of a neglected building — moored in midtown like an obsolete liner awaiting the breakers — for a brave new city plaza with gardens and fountains seemed an attractive bargain at first. But gradually awareness of history and heritage and the possibility of restoration pushed back the bulldozers. The QVB found friends after its wilderness years. Public meetings, letters to editors, the National Trust and the Royal Australian Institute of Architects (NSW chapter) rallied support in the rescue campaign. They urged that the building be preserved but none had a credible suggestion for financing restoration. In 1969 a candidate in the Council elections said that if elected he would propose demolition. He was not elected.

In 1971 the first decade of debate ended when the Mayor, Alderman Emmet McDermott, announced that the QVB would be reprieved and restored. The actor-writer Barry Humphries saluted this decision with a poem praising the Council's 'wisdom and vision'. In 1973 another admirer, the Sydney novelist Ruth Park, wrote that 'one of the great sights' of Sydney was also 'one of the most argued-about, most-hated, and most-loved buildings' in the city. Another decade was to pass before an economically viable role was discovered for the QVB, one that would ensure that its future would be founded on something sounder than sentiment.

The top floor at the commencement of renovation in 1984 showing remnants of the 1930s alterations. The structure which supported the false ceiling under the barrel vault is evident, and the concrete infills of the gallery voids have yet to be removed. Sheets of corrugated iron which replaced the original glass have been removed to allow light to stream in.

Photograph Jenny Blain.

Following page: The interior nearing completion in March 1986.

Photograph John Witzig.

Throughout the 1970s, scores of proposals — for hotels, arts centres, apartments, casinos — were made by Australian and overseas groups. But only one, Stephenson & Turner's 1976 plan to restore the derelict building to its original use as a mixed retail centre met the requirements of the City Council, the Heritage Council, the National Trust and the community as a whole. The Town Clerk, Mr Leon Carter, said that what was wanted next was a 'wealthy visionary'.

In 1980 that essential element entered the QVB saga in the form of Ipoh Garden Berhad, a Malaysian public company with interests in Singapore, Hong Kong and the United States as well as Australia. (Ipoh's co-founder, Dato Tan Chin Nam, was well-known in Australia as an owner of Think Big, winner of the Melbourne Cup in 1974 and 1975.) In 1980, seeking further opportunities in Australia, the Ipoh group with the support of the Council of the City of Sydney assembled the project team and instructed Rice & Daubney, Stephenson & Turner as joint architects to prepare the necessary designs.

In 1982 the City Council and Ipoh Garden Berhad agreed on a 99-year lease and profit-sharing contract. Since then the company has invested some $75 million to turn back the clock to an elegant era and at the same time prepare the QVB to prosper far into a third century.

The gallery void stripped to her bare essentials
(above) and *(right)* with some of her finery on.
Photographs Jenny Templin.

The QVB, open for business and a
new future.
Photograph David Moore.

In 1986, the grand old lady is still intact — and once
again shining as she did in 1898.

Photograph (opposite) David Moore.

Photograph (above) Mitchell Library.

THE 1890s

THE Queen Victoria Building, as its name proclaims, was built in the heyday of British imperial influence in Australia. It was an era of rapid economic and social improvement, an age of optimism, a favourite word of the period. It was also a time of historic political change in Australia. The 1890s were crowded with the signs of the ending of an era and portents of the birth of a nation.

In those years, as the eloquent nationalist leader Sir Henry Parkes put it, 'the crimson thread of kinship' tied the Australian colonies to Britain. Ninety-eight per cent of Australia's population of 3.5 million was of English, Irish, Scottish or Welsh descent. Yet in the 1890s Australians moved, cautiously at first, then quickly, in a series of political conferences and referenda, from colonial status towards independent nationhood. It would take them many more years to complete the process, but the first fundamental steps were swift.

At the beginning of the decade, the six British colonies covering the continent were united mainly by fervent loyalty to the distant and seemingly immortal monarch who gave her name to the era and to the great Sydney market building.

Queen Victoria had reigned over the British Empire for most of the century. Between 1855 and 1870, she signed separate grants of provincial self-government for the six colonies into which geographical Australia was divided. For a further generation, the colonies seemed satisfied with this restricted role in the worldwide imperial family on which the sun never set. 'Rule Britannia' was

sung with passion on public occasions. The colonies eagerly volunteered soldiers to fight in remote British quarrels such as the Sudan rising (1885), the Boer War and the Boxer Rebellion (both 1899). Australia's coins bore images of Victoria and Britannia. Two-thirds of imports were marked 'British made' and most exports went in British ships to British shops.

Three-quarters of the stocks and bonds in Australia were owned by British investors. Australia's flag was the Union Jack. In the words of one historian, 'Such dependence on Britain could well have been resented by Australians if they had not been so British themselves.'

Not everyone was reverent about the Empire and British royalty. The republican *Bulletin* derided royalists as 'Union Jackals' and called the Empire 'The British Vampire'. The most outspoken anti-monarchist was John Norton, the flamboyant editor of the muckraking *Truth*, a Sydney weekly often more concerned with sensation than with facts. Norton, later a member of the City Council, was one of Sydney's wilder eccentrics, forever in the courts and bars of the litigious, hard-drinking city. He was, among other things, the inventor of the epithet 'wowser', an insult he applied to his many enemies, including rival aldermen.

Norton had been printing insults about Queen Victoria and the Royal family for years, but in 1896 one of his articles strained government tolerance too far. He had denounced as 'slavish sycophancy' proposals for special ceremonies to mark 23 September, the day on which Victoria became the longest-reigning

Circular Quay, Sydney, in 1885 — the N.S.W.
contingent to the Sudan War prepare to embark.

Photograph N.S.W. Government Printer.

monarch in British history. The Queen, wrote Norton, was a 'semi-senile, sulky-faced little German woman' whose ancestors, he claimed, had been madmen and lechers. The prosecution claimed that this 'wickedly, maliciously and seditiously' vilified Her Majesty, 'held her up to ridicule, hatred, and contempt', and was 'a crime against society'. Norton was charged with sedition, a form of treason.

As erudite as he was reckless, he conducted his own defence, quoting dozens of legal and literary references from memory. He concluded, 'I am a loyal Australian and a republican.' He impressed or confused the jury so much that they failed to agree on a verdict and the case was dropped. This was a triumph for Norton and, ironically, soon afterwards it helped him to win election to the City Council, a stronghold of monarchists.

But the political temper of the times was seldom so fierce. Australian nationalism was increasing in strength, but it did not exclude a place in the Empire. The campaigns for Federation — the uniting of the colonies as a new nation with a federal parliament — were not anti-British. Indeed, when the century closed with Queen Victoria signing legislation to create the Commonwealth of Australia, the new nation was not as a result any less British, nor even particularly independent of Britain. A London cartoon of the time aptly depicted the new nation as an animal with the body of a kangaroo and the head of a lion. The British government had conceded enough authority to satisfy the main nationalist leaders, Edmund Barton, the Sydney lawyer who

became the first Prime Minister, and Alfred Deakin, the Melbourne journalist who was the first Attorney-General. But Britain retained enough powers to reassure those Australians who also cherished Britannia's rule.

For both camps, there were many memorable ceremonies at the turn of the century. Among the many loyal tributes on the Queen's Diamond Jubilee in 1897, the sixtieth anniversary of her accession to the throne, the Sydney City Council named its New Market Building, still under construction, in her honour.

On the first day of the new century there was a strong British flavour to the celebrations of the birth of federal Australia. Eleven warships of the Royal Navy sailed into Sydney Harbour. One thousand elite British troops — Guards, Hussars, Fusiliers — marched in the eight-kilometre-long procession through the city to Centennial Park for the proclamation of the new nation. (As Barton put it, 'For the first time in history, we have a continent for a nation, and a nation for a continent.')

Queen Victoria's representative and Australia's first Governor-General, the Earl of Hopetoun, rode in an open carriage, touching his plumed hat to the enormous crowds, estimated at 250,000. The cheering throngs, sweltering in the midsummer heat, were particularly packed along George Street from Martin Place to the Queen Victoria Building. The new building was decked with flags and red, white and blue bunting. Rudyard Kipling, the favourite bard of Empire, celebrated the great occasion with a purple poem hailing the new Commonwealth as 'Queen of

Tom Roberts with his painting of the opening of the
first federal parliament in Melbourne's Exhibition
Building.
Photograph Mitchell Library.

The rat incinerator used in the extermination campaign during an outbreak of bubonic plague in Sydney.

Photograph N.S.W. Government Printer.

the Sovereign South'. As Deakin recorded, that night Sydney celebrated with 'tremendous uproar' in the streets, where 'whistles, bells, gongs, rattles, and clanging cutlery yielded unearthly sounds'.

Just three weeks later, the old Queen was dead. The Victorian era was over after sixty-three years, and her Empire went into mourning. Australia, fresh from festivities, was shocked into official and individual sorrow. Public buildings, the QVB the largest of them, were draped in black and purple crepe, and flags, still flying from the Federation celebrations, were lowered to half-mast.

Next, in this long season of sentiment and symbolism, came civic gatherings to mark the accession to the throne of Victoria's son. Among the first actions of the new King, Edward VII, was to despatch his son, the Duke of York, to Australia. Dressed as a British admiral, the Duke of York formally opened the first federal parliament. Melbourne was the venue, not simply because its rival, Sydney, had staged the proclamation of the nation, but because only Melbourne had a hall, the Exhibition Building, large enough to hold the 14,000 people who managed to be invited. Tom Roberts came down from his Sydney studio to record the historic scene. The painting, five metres by three metres, had a typical Australian-British history. It was begun in Melbourne, finished in London, presented by the new Australian government to the new King and finally returned to Australia by his granddaughter Queen Elizabeth.

Against this background of politics and pageantry, of nationalists and royalists, late-Victorian Sydney was a dynamic city, growing and changing rapidly. In thirty years its population

had trebled to almost half a million. After London, Sydney was the largest 'white' city of the British Empire. It was a centre of world commerce; trade across the harbour wharves had increased threefold in twenty years to five million tonnes a year.

Apart from the numbers in the ledgers, there was architectural proof of prosperity. Buildings told the city's story, too. New suburbs of terraces, cottages and villas followed the spreading spokes of the tram and rail networks. In the 1000-hectare downtown district, commerce built hundreds of substantial and sometimes stylish offices, department stores and warehouses. Banks, insurers, shipowners, woolbrokers, retailers and other merchant princes took over much of the cityscape, establishing its shape for the next fifty years.

New techniques for higher-rise construction, such as steel framing and hydraulic lifts, suddenly lifted average new building heights from two and three storeys to six or eight, changing a skyline previously punctuated only by church spires and municipal clock towers. George and Pitt and other central streets became canyons of sandstone and granite. The last wooden buildings vanished.

The late-Victorian construction boom — not surpassed until the 1960s — did not aspire to the serene Georgian elegance of Sydney's colonial legacy of convict-built churches, houses and barracks. But many were handsome and some monumental.

Among the best or best known of these Victorian visual gifts, with their stone, iron and sculpted elegance and

The Paddington Cricket Club's First Eleven for the season 1897-98. Victor Trumper is seated on the far left, with M. A. Nobel second from the right in the back row.

Photograph Mitchell Library.

Coogee Beach in the 1890s.

Photograph Mitchell Library.

The elaborate Fish Market in Woolloomooloo circa 1870.

Photograph Mitchell Library.

The almost-completed Sydney Town Hall loomed
above the George Street Markets in the late 1880s.
Photograph N.S.W. Government Printer.

eccentricities, were the Lands Department Building (1874), Town Hall (1888), Post Office (1890), CML Building (1894), Strand Arcade (1892), the cathedrals of St Andrew and St Mary (1868 and 1882) the Great Synagogue (1874), such mercantile palaces as the Huddart Parks and Burns Philp buildings of the 1880s and such hotels as the Metropole and Pfahlerts.

Victorian Sydney had one disadvantage for builders, which persists; its unplanned convict-era streets are too narrow to show off the architecture. There were no broad boulevard views, as there are in Melbourne and Adelaide which are laid out like chessboards. Then as now, Sydney was a place of views to and from the harbour.

Sydney had also become a favourite port of call for world travellers, entertainers and writers. Notable visitors to Sydney in the 1890s included Mark Twain, Sarah Bernhardt, Robert Louis Stevenson, Rudyard Kipling, British racing writer Nat Gould, and John L. Sullivan (as an actor, after his career as a bare-knuckle boxer). Another regular visitor to the port was a young Anglo-Polish ship's officer, Joseph Conrad, who left the sea soon afterwards to write of the Pacific and other oceans.

Despite the staid atmosphere we glimpse today in the sepia-tinted photographs of the 1890s — which are such popular collectibles in the nostalgic 1980s — there was already in Sydney the taste of the twentieth century and its technology. Winds of change were blowing as steadily as the summer northeasters.

Australia had been linked to London by overland and undersea telegraph since 1872, and in the 1880s a few large offices installed the telephone. In the 1890s other electro-mechanical marvels appeared. One was a machine whose first models resembled 'a cross between a sewing machine and a galvanic battery' — the era of Edison had arrived with the phonograph and 'graphophone' on whose first wax cylinders was recorded, among other music, the voice of Dame Nellie Melba, who had just made her New York debut.

In 1894 another American wonder, the kinetoscope, was demonstrated in Sydney. This flicked photographs before a lens at forty frames a second to show 'objects in motion as in real life'. The moving picture was not far away. In 1896 the Tivoli theatre alternated music hall acts with M. Lumiere's amazing new *cinematographe*, fresh from Paris. It screened the first movie made in Australia — a newsreel of that year's Melbourne Cup, won by Newhaven. Anticipating the invention of television by some forty years, a reporter observed that if the telegraph could be connected to the *cinematographe* 'the public could on Cup Day see the race as it progresses'. The other notable picture taken that year was the first Australian X-ray, only three months after the invention of radiography.

In 1894, Sydney inventor Lawrence Hargrave, whose face is on the $20 note, made an historic experimental flight, lifted by complex kites whose novel shapes later helped the Wright brothers to design the wings of the first powered aircraft.

Just before Christmas 1899, Sydney's first electric tram rumbled and sparked past the Queen Victoria Building heralding

the century of electronics.

True, in 1899 the everyday sights and sounds of the city still included hansom and hackney cabs (there were 1312), horsedrawn buses (287), and sixty kilometres of track for steam trams. At Circular Quay, wool was loaded in tall clipper ships and fast steamers. The ferry to Manly was a paddle-wheeler. The glow and glare of gas lamps lit the city.

But horse, steam, gas, sail, and iron were giving ground to the advance of electricity, steel, petrol, elevators and motor cars (of which there were twenty in Sydney by 1899).

In high fashion, the rustle of the bustle, which had replaced the creak of the crinoline, was receding. New dresses featured enormous leg-o'-mutton sleeves (appropriate at a time of mutton-chop whiskers). Less formal ladies donned knickerbockers, known as 'rational dress', to join the craze for the new safety bicycle, a favourite subject for another invention newly on sale, the roll-film box camera of which the posters of Messrs Kodak promised: 'You press the button — we'll do the rest.'

The new gowns and gadgets crowded the shelves of the great Sydney emporiums — David Jones, Farmer's, Mark Foy's, Grace Bros, Marcus Clark's, Hordern's. These dukes of drapery expanded fast in the 1890s. In 1896, for instance, Hordern's, whose main showroom was 100 metres long, employed 4000 people, served six million customers across its counters and delivered two million parcels in its own horse-drawn vans.

These retailing dynasties made no great architectural mark on the city (although Farmer's had introduced plate glass to Australia as early as 1873). It was not until the concept of the shopping arcade or galleria, originally Middle Eastern and refined in Milan, reached Sydney that retailing contributed influential, distinctive buildings.

In London the Burlington Arcade off Piccadilly had proved a commercial and fashionable success, and in Moscow in 1890 a 300-metre arcade on Red Square was rising. (After the Russian Revolution, it became the GUM department store.)

Sydney entrepreneurs, always seeking something new, seized on the idea and in the 1890s built a series of lofty, ornate glass-roofed arcades in the city centre, housing hundreds of new shops. The largest had resounding names befitting their image of a transplanted London West End — the Strand , the Victoria, the Imperial and the Royal. The Strand Arcade, built in 1892, survives — restored to its former glory in 1978 by the architects Stephenson & Turner — but the others gave way eventually to tower blocks or were converted beyond recognition. They were instantly successful; all Sydney flocked to marvel at their marble and to promenade under their chandeliers, shaped for the era of gaslight but, increasingly, illuminated by electricity.

In short, everything was up to date in Sydney city and they had gone about as far as they could go. Well, not quite. There were also slums, sweat shops and strikes — and the sewers were not ideal. Inevitably in a big, competitive, commercial city — born of booms in gold, wool, immigration, land, coal, construction, transport and manufacturing — there were great contrasts 'of wealth and poverty, of palace and slum, of commercial efficiency and civic ineptitude', as a writer of the period put it. But as Michael Cannon, the prominent modern historian of Victorian Australia, writes, 'Urban life might be frequently harsh and unfair by today's standards, but it was never dull, not ever.' Sydney had also enjoyed a whole generation of economic growth. By 1900 its living standards were, as economists later calculated, higher than those of Britain or the United States. One of the great symbols and monuments of this age of optimism and improvement — and of eager technology — was the Queen Victoria Building. And as the era closed, the QVB opened its ornate gates to a new and more complex century.

Above: The Garden Palace, built in the Botanical Gardens for the Sydney International Exposition 1879-80, was destroyed by fire in 1882.

Photograph Mitchell Library.

Right: The parasol, ribbon and lace department in David Jones department store circa 1890.

Photograph David Jones.

MACQUARIE TO McRAE

T HE story of the Queen Victoria Building is, in part, the story of two Scots: Lachlan Macquarie and George McRae. They were born almost a century apart, Macquarie in 1761, McRae in 1858, but their places in the history of the QVB are clearly and directly linked. In 1810 Macquarie, Governor of the colony of New South Wales, established the first city market square. At the end of the century McRae, the City Architect, built on the same site the majestic market hall that Macquarie, a great builder and a patron of architecture, would surely have admired.

Among Macquarie's many legacies to Sydney are its finest Georgian buildings. MacRae's monument is the QVB, which speaks as clearly of the Victorian era. Macquarie had commanded construction of a public hospital (part of which has become the New South Wales Parliament Building) and financed it, ironically, by giving the builders licences to import rum. He appointed, at a wage of three shillings a day, the first official architect, Francis Greenway, a convicted forger, and even named a Poet Laureate, Michael Robinson, who had been transported to Botany Bay for blackmail.

The best-loved city building of Macquarie's tenure (1810-22) is St James's Church, designed by Greenway. Its graceful spire was the main distinction of the Sydney skyline until McRae's spectacular main dome of the QVB was completed in 1898.

Macquarie straightened, widened and named as streets the rutted tracks straggling across his sprawling village (the capital of a colony as big as half of Europe). One he named for himself,

another for his wife, Elizabeth, the others for various British royals and nobles. A track, popularly known as 'Sergeant Major's Row', which began where the Rocks tumbled down to Sydney Cove, became George Street. At first the 'street' was less imposing than its name. Macquarie found it occupied along the waterfront by an untidy daily market where produce, livestock, and poultry were bargained and bartered with rum as currency. The piles of vegetables and poultry pens also hindered access to King's Wharf, the colony's main landing place, and encroached on the nearby parade ground of the garrison, the 73rd Regiment of Foot.

Macquarie, reasonably enough, considered a market from which livestock wandered under the boots of his redcoats as 'very badly and inconveniently situated'. He ordered it moved almost two kilometres inland to 'a more commodious situation'. This was on the edge of his little township, a paddock 'part of which was lately used by Mr Blaxland as a stockyard'. This was bounded on the east by George Street, on the west by newly-named York Street, and on the south by the 'Burial Ground', the colony's first cemetery (now the site of the Sydney Town Hall). The northern boundary Macquarie called Market Street, and he ordered it marked out west to Cockle Bay, now Darling Harbour. There, his convict carpenters and stonemasons built a wharf 'for the convenience of those bringing grain and other merchandise in boats from the Hawkesbury to the new market place'.

Although Macquarie's first town-planning decision was farsighted — a produce market flourished on the site for almost

Above: The interior of the George Street Market.
Photograph Tyrell Collection — ACP.

Left: The domed Market House on Druitt Street was designed by Macquarie's convict architect Francis Greenway.
Photograph N.S.W. Government Printer.

a century — it would lead him, within a few years, into an official argument, a difficulty not unknown to later administrators of the site.

The first market buildings put up on the paddock of Mr Blaxland (who went off to win fame as a pioneer of a route through the Blue Mountains) was a simple storehouse and office of rough planks and logs. But Macquarie and his eager architect Francis Greenway had ambitious plans for the area.

Greenway envisaged a grand civic square anchored on the market place and flanked by a cathedral, a town hall and a government hotel. Macquarie laid only a foundation stone for St Andrew's (although construction did not begin for another twenty years) and not until 1820 was Greenway's market office begun. It was a handsome, two-storey brick and stone building with neoclassic pillars and portico, a domed central roof some ten metres high and a spire with a weathercock.

But London vetoed the civic square buildings and market halls. The British government considered that Sydney should be little more than 'a place of punishment' and opposed Macquarie's lofty civic ambitions, as well as his scandalous habit of mixing freely with convicts and ex-convicts.

After Macquarie's departure the market office was converted into a police station and magistrate's court, although the market behind it still thrived in wooden sheds. The facilities also included a pillory and whipping post for the public punishment of those convicted by the magistrates next door. The nearest gallows was nearby in Park Street, and if that was occupied there was another

in George Street where the Regent Hotel now stands.

As Sydney's population of immigrants and 'emancipists' (ex-convicts) increased, better markets were needed. In the 1830s, when the population was about twenty thousand, four substantial stone halls were built on the site by immigrant Scottish tradesmen, directed by Mr Brodie, to the design of Government Architect Ambrose Hallen. Each was sixty metres long and ten metres wide, divided into stalls selling produce, poultry and meat, set around a paved square. A visitor in 1839 wrote: 'From the elegance of its appearance it bespeaks an amphitheatre rather than a public market'.

In 1842, when Sydney Town was incorporated as a city and had a population of about thirty-five thousand, the first Council took over the markets, establishing the municipal control of the site maintained to this day.

The Council set the market hours as sunrise to sunset, with 'late shopping' until 10 pm on Wednesdays and 11.30 pm on Saturdays. Stall rents were between two shillings and six shillings a week, cash in advance, with fines up to forty shillings for anyone leaving rubbish around.

From 1859 to 1869 the Council made further improvements, extending the stalls, building an office with a decorative tower at the Market Street entrance and roofing over the entire square. In this form the George Street Markets, which had started as Mr Blaxland's stockyard and which had acquired neighbours as prestigious as the cathedral and town hall envisioned by Governor

Far left: As early as the 1890s there was a proposal for a park on the site of the George Street Markets. *Mitchell Library.*

Left: George McRae had other plans; he presented four sets of elevations to the City Council.

Below: McRae's Queen Anne option. *Photograph and drawing Mitchell Library.*

ELEVATION TO GEORGE STREET, SYDNEY

The Mayor of Sydney, S. L. Lees, laying a corner-
stone of what was then known as the New City
Markets.

Photograph Mitchell Library.

Macquarie, were a Sydney landmark for another generation.

Then in 1888 the City Architect George McRae entered the history of the markets with plans far grander than those of their first architect, Francis Greenway.

Victorian Sydney had boomed since the gold discoveries of the 1850s and through the phenomenal growth of the wool trade (flocks more than doubled to 100 million in the twenty years to 1891) and much of its commercial core was established near the old markets. In Market Street was the department store of Farmer Bros and George Street was the headquarters of the Hordern and David Jones dynasties. In 1889, the adjacent Town Hall had added its Centennial Hall, then the largest municipal concert hall in the world. In contrast, the old market and police buildings of architects Greenway and Hallen were looking distinctly dowdy by the 1880s.

The City Council was almost totally lacking in social concern (its sewerage and public health services were a disgrace), but it was strong on civic pride and enjoyed an edifice complex. Sydney had recently lost its flashiest public building, the government's ornate Garden Palace, which had been destroyed by fire. A few months later the City Council began considering raising something spectacular of its own — not necessarily because the Garden Palace had been lost (though the coincidence was certainly intriguing). And in the decaying markets the Council had an inviting, almost irresistible site.

The Garden Palace had been Sydney's extravagant response to Melbourne's Exhibition Building, itself a loud and lasting echo of the Crystal Palace built in London in 1851. The Garden Palace was rushed up at a cost of £191,000 in only eight months on two hectares of the Botanical Gardens for the Sydney International Exhibition of 1879-80. This was an enormous exposition of trade, agriculture and industry which attracted tens of thousands of local, British, American, European, and Asian exhibits and more than a million visitors in its seven months.

The *Sydney Morning Herald* described the sprawling pavilions of timber, glass and iron as 'like a fabled palace in the Arabian Nights'. In fact, it was nearer to baroque than to Baghdad. With its towers, turrets, domes and other pretensions, it was a building of a thousand and one styles.

The Garden Palace and its fate were significant not only for business, the lifeblood of Sydney, but also for innovation in architecture and construction. The building gave a boost to the commercial use of electricity: in the rush to build it workers had, for the first time, laboured at night by the light provided by portable gas-powered generators. Australia's first passenger lifts were another wonder of the Garden Palace. Installed by an American company to promote sales, the steam-powered lifts were dismantled after the great show and sold to Toohey's brewery. A year later Farmer Bros' Pitt Street store installed a fancier, cable-operated version, and Sydney buildings began to shoot upwards to take advantage of these elevating inventions. This, in turn, required the introduction of concrete and steel. The blaze at the Garden Palace

Left: **The centre dome under construction.**
Photograph Mitchell Library.

Below: **The corner of George and Market Streets showing the ground level nearing completion.**
Photograph National Trust.

and the fear of fire in the newer, taller buildings, led to the introduction of early forms of fireproofing using terracotta or concrete.

After the exhibition, the Garden Palace was put to a mixture of uses as varied as its appearance — for concerts, balls, for keeping government records and, pending completion of the State art gallery, for display and storage of paintings. The fire that swept the building at dawn on 22 September 1882 destroyed many records of the New South Wales census of 1881 and some of Sydney's earliest archives, leading to popular suspicion of arson by prosperous descendants of convicts anxious to be rid of embarrassing family trees.

The blaze, reported the *Herald,* was 'the most spectacular ever seen in Australia . . . a gigantic firework'. The heat cracked windows in nearby Macquarie Street and when the main dome of iron over flimsy wooden frames collapsed, a fireball erupted, hurling galvanised sheets for kilometres. Several chunks fell into a garden in Elizabeth Bay.

Somehow a few paintings survived although, as the *Herald* observed, some of the hundreds destroyed 'are not to be regretted'. One whose destruction would have been regretted was 'Chloe', an oil painting by Le Febure of an ample young woman whose nudity had caused some controversy at the French exhibit two years earlier. But 'Chloe' had already made her way from the Garden Palace to Melbourne, where she found fame in the saloon bar of Young and Jackson's Hotel.

The Garden Palace is now little more than a fiery footnote in the history of Victorian Sydney, but while it lasted the city was inordinately proud of it, although a few toffs with apartments on fashionable Macquarie Street complained that it blocked their drawing-room views of the harbour. In provincial grief, the *Herald* claimed that 'the whole of the civilised world' heard 'with regret' of its destruction. Anyone producing another public building with such style on such a scale would obviously have gained kudos.

The following year the City Council asked its Architect, Thomas Sapsford, to plan a replacement for the decaying George Street markets. He was busy, with his assistant George McRae, on the troublesome construction of the Town Hall auditorium and apparently he drafted nothing on the markets before his death in 1887. McRae, who had arrived from Edinburgh three years before, became City Architect at the age of only twenty-eight.

From Scotland he had carried an employer's reference predicting, 'You will be certain to make your mark in the country of your adoption'. McRae's mark was to be the Queen Victoria Building. In 1888 he published, in the *Building and Engineering Journal,* a draft design which predated by five years his final plan for the QVB. The *Journal,* which naturally pushed any bricks-and-mortar barrow it could get hold of, was agitating for the demolition of the old markets, citing the developers' familiar grounds of public welfare and sensible economics — adding that demolition would be a good thing 'from an artistic point of view'. Its editor's concern for aesthetics did not, however, extend to replacing the markets

The newly completed glass-roofed barrel vault from the upper gallery level.

Photograph Mitchell Library.

with a square or gardens, as some councillors had suggested. The *Journal* said, reasonably enough, that Sydney was 'already tolerably well provided with public parks'. No, what was needed was to clear away the old markets which had become 'miserable', 'utterly inadequate' and a 'disgrace' and build something better and larger which the city could rent 'with the probability of considerable profit'.

McRae's sketch plans were for a building some 400 feet (120 metres) long and 115 feet (35 metres) wide with facades in the fussy, pretty Queen Anne style, topped with turrets and gables. The interior was a lofty, spacious hall rising from market and shop levels to a glass roof. The *Journal* suggested adding galleries to increase the rentable floor space. That comment and the design of the galleried Strand Arcade, built a little later, might well have influenced McRae when he went back to the drawing board in October 1892 with instructions from the Mayor to quickly produce a selection of sketch plans for new George Street markets.

The Sydney City Council was fifty years old at this time. The only older institutions in the state were the Bank of New South Wales (1817), now Westpac, and the *Sydney Morning Herald* (1837). The Council was well set in its ways. Its wings have since been somewhat clipped by state governments, but it was then a strong-willed and secretive body, not amenable to public scrutiny or outside opinions. On the issue of the markets, it made a series of decisions that were at best high-handed and at worst downright foolish or, to be charitable, over-optimistic. The Council decided to demolish the old markets, buy the adjoining police station to enlarge the site, build a new market complex, borrow money for the works, ignore advice on the markets' location, and not to consult outside architects.

It was a bold approach and, in terms of getting an impressive building up on time and on budget, it was remarkably efficient. It might have been more diplomatic of the Council to hold a design competition among prominent architects but, in the event, McRae offered plenty to choose from. Why a new city market had spending priority over public health was not explained — and it took a deadly outbreak of bubonic plague a few years later to force the Council to spend more on sewers and drains. A delegation of produce dealers had asked the Council to relocate the markets to a site near Darling Harbour. They were ignored.

The Council gave no economic justification for its decisions to replace the old markets. Indeed, there were none. There was no town plan or town planners. Municipal decisions were a mixture of strong wills, whims of iron, grand gestures and aldermanic interests. True, the markets were 'unsightly', as the Council said, but they were no more 'unsightly' than the inner-city slums which the Council had been ignoring for years. The difference was that the slums were a short walk away from the Town Hall but the offending markets could be seen from the aldermanic chambers. True, some market tenants had left — ironically for the new Belmore Markets which the Council had just built further along George Street.

In 1898 she stood in all her magnificent splendour.
Street level shop windows were required by law to be
covered on Sundays.

Photograph Mitchell Library.

The spiral staircase leading to the centre dome.
Photograph Mitchell Library.

The Council moved through this thicket of contradictions and loose ends with little more reason than the warm, inner glow given by the Victorian belief in continuous material progress. In short, the QVB was built not by logic but by faith — as were the Taj Mahal, the Sphinx and other splendid follies.

Indeed, if the Council had chosen to test its instincts against economic analyses and market research, it is highly probable that the QVB would not have been built. Sydney owes it to the conceit and myopia of the City Councils of the 1890s whose other notable legacy was the death of the 107 citizens in the bubonic plague epidemic of 1900.

The opportunity for the Council to make its grand gesture on George Street was clinched when the state government decided to vacate the police and magistrates' offices in Greenway's old building beside the market. In 1892 the Council agreed to pay £124,000 for the land. This added two hundred feet (sixty metres) to the council-owned market site, presenting McRae with the challenge of a tricky shape and space — a long, narrow rectangle some one hundred and eighty metres long by just under thirty metres wide. He seized the opportunity with the energy of a man given the chance of a lifetime and rushed a selection of sketches to the Council — sketches of the *interior* possibilities of marketing buildings. The exteriors could wait. He put function ahead of facade.

The Council's response on 17 October 1892 was virtually a blank cheque. It said simply that the building should have a basement and three storeys and that McRae's outlines of a long, galleried arcade were suitable. The most ambitious architectural and construction undertaking in Australian history to that date was launched with breathtaking speed and confidence. The stereotypes of dour Scot and stuffy Victorian aldermen did not fit young McRae and his municipal masters. True, Aldermen Hughes and Harris sounded notes of caution by proposing that 'competitive designs be invited . . . to obtain the best plans that could possibly be had' and to give the Council 'the benefit of all the experience' available. This suggestion, which would have meant delay, was brushed aside by a Council vote of 15 to 4. The demolishers had already cleared the site of the visible evidence of the Macquarie-Greenway era. With his consultant engineer George Massey, McRae then wrote specifications for excavations before he had decided in detail what was to go in them. And the Council let a £10,000 contract for preparation of the site before it had raised the money to build on it, and before McRae had designed what was to be built.

However, the pieces of the gigantic jigsaw fell smoothly and surely into place. Excavations began in March 1893. In July, McRae gave the Council a choice of four exterior designs and a selection was made; in the same month there were preparations to call tenders for the superstructure. In August documents for a loan of £300,000 were drafted and in September tenders for the superstructure were called. On 25 November a £5,000 contract for it was signed, on the same day McRae's final design was

George Street at the intersection of King Street
looking south to the QVB around the turn of the
century.
Photograph Tyrrell Collection — ACP.

Stairs at the York Street entrance led to the galleries.
Photograph Mitchell Library.

exhibited at the Town Hall and on 15 December the foundation stone was laid.

The stone was suitably massive. As the five-tonne block of granite was levered and lowered into position at the corner of George and Druitt streets, the Mayor, William Manning, gave it a ceremonial pat with a silver trowel presented to him by the excavation contractors as a souvenir of the occasion. (The trowel surfaced at a Sydney auction in 1986 and was bought by an antique dealer for $2000.) The ceremony was the first of a series in which successive mayors laid stones and plaques to mark the progress of construction and to ensure that their names were inscribed on their municipal monument.

In September 1895, with the iron and steel superstructures finished and the masons taking over, the new Mayor, S.E. Lees, laid a corner stone at the intersection of George and Market streets. His successor, I.E. Ives, was more adventurous when his moment of glory came in July 1896. With the facades of Waverley sandstone almost complete, he climbed the scaffolding high above the archway of the George Street entrance to set a stone recording his role. From that vantage point he had a fine view of the half-hectare or so of stone, steel and bricks, iron, concrete and glass which McRae and the contractors were bringing together.

If Alderman Ives, or indeed anyone among the crowds of passers-by who daily watched the busy spectacle for more than five years, had been asked to describe the shape and style of what was emerging, they might have had difficulty — or, at least, offered

different descriptions. For although the QVB has generated as many words as the Harbour Bridge or the Opera House, it has also often left observers at a loss for words, or struggling to find the right ones. The innumerable descriptions attempted have suggested a palatial combination of English guildhall, Italianate galleria, Islamic bazaar and Victorian arcade with elaborate facades and features labelled from time to time as American Romanesque, Byzantine, or simply High Victorian. Perhaps the truth is that the QVB resists precise description because it is unique, a singular mixture of ideas and influences combined perhaps at random, and certainly with daring. Morton Herman, the noted historian of Australian architecture, says that in the period when the QVB was commissioned by the Council and designed by McRae 'the philosophy of architecture was in a state of confusion'. No one school or style predominated in Sydney's building boom, so McRae presented the Council with not one but four designs, offering them the same building in four styles — one Gothic in character, one Renaissance, one Queen Anne and one Romanesque. The *Australian Builder and Contractor's News* in July 1893 said the Renaissance design was the 'most scholarly' and the Gothic the 'least engaging'. The journal said the Queen Anne version was 'picturesque', although 'without exaggeration'. The Council chose the Romanesque version despite what the journal called its 'rather startling' surplus of domes. The traditional appearances McRae offered were deceptive because he intended them to contain much that was new. As Morton Herman has written, McRae was not

50

The wonderful interior.
Photograph Mitchell Library.

The central arches at the first floor level.
Photograph Mitchell Library.

only a 'well-informed and bold designer' but also 'one of the leading protagonists' of the new construction methods and materials which were then 'beginning to break down the conservatism of building techniques'.

By the standards of the day, McRae's building was high-tech as well as High Victorian, although its exterior revealed nothing of the advanced ideas within. There was a construction revolution going on and McRae took a primary role in it. Professor James Freeland, the architect and historian, has written that the 'unique and tremendous significance' for architecture of the 1890s was the introduction of new methods and materials. For instance, in McRae's plans for the Belmore and Woolloomooloo market halls in 1892-93, he designed light steel roof frames and trusses which were novel then and whose technique was standard for another sixty years. And McRae's next project, the QVB, was the showpiece of his ingenuity and innovation in construction.

In achieving the strength and space of the building, McRae used steel, iron, concrete, reinforcing, machine-made bricks, glass, imported tiles, fire-proofing, riveting and hydraulics on an unprecedented scale. Like the Harbour Bridge and the Opera House, the QVB was of great technical and professional interest to engineers, architects and builders. Some of its statistics — the 4.5 million bricks, the 3000 tonnes of iron and steel, the half-hectare of glass, the mountains of sandstone and granite —

attracted popular interest. But what made McRae's masterpiece the wonder of the day to most Sydneysiders — the average citizens on the George Street tram — was the look of the thing. They marvelled at its style rather than its substance. As the central dome and its cupola rose triumphantly to sixty metres above the streets, civic pride soared with them.

The City Council decided that such grandeur deserved a regal name. The choice was obvious. In 1897, before the whole work was finished, the Council declared it to be the Queen Victoria Market Building — certainly a more imposing name than 'the George Street New Markets' and a timely tribute from the most distant of her domains to a monarch completing the sixtieth year of her record reign.

The making of the QVB was also the making of McRae. Even before the official opening in 1898, he was approached by the state government with the irresistible offer of the post of Assistant New South Wales Architect. This was a promotion which, he rightly calculated, would surely lead him to become Government Architect. There was a fine flourish of history in this. For the post was first held by Francis Greenway who had designed for Macquarie the first Sydney market building on the very same site. The ghost of Lachlan Macquarie, a Scot who, like McRae, left his mark on Australia, might well have smiled on such a fitting event.

The lift which carried produce and vehicles from
York Street to the basement livestock, fruit and
vegetable market.
Photograph Mitchell Library.

NO WAY TO TREAT A LADY

ON the afternoon of Thursday 21 July 1898, exactly ten years after George McRae had published his first plans, the Queen Victoria Building was formally opened. After four years and eight months of construction, it was time for the speechmaking. At the ceremonies the Lord Mayor of Sydney, Alderman Matthew Harris, declared it was 'a magnificent pile of buildings'. That was a blunt but fitting description, for the scale and strength of the QVB suggested it might have been put up by the same company that did Stonehenge.

Certainly, it looked built to last. 'It may be truly said that we have here built for the future as well as the present,' the Lord Mayor said. He added, with a mixture of prescience and pride, 'This is a work that will live with the centuries and stand as a landmark in history, speaking to people yet unborn of our commercial, social and material existence. It is no exaggeration to state that south of the line there is no public building that either for size, beauty, or utility can compare with this noble edifice — it will be viewed by citizens and visitors as an architectural triumph of this century.' After that bit of backslapping, reasonable enough on a day of celebration, the Mayor gave the first official explanation of the reason for the QVB's being on such an enormous scale. The reasons he gave were philosophical as well as practical.

Alderman Harris said that the QVB was intended to be far more than a municipal market. He said, 'A less costly building would have provided ample market accommodation. But it would have been short-sighted to have only studied the present to the exclusion of that great future which far-seeing men agree will be almost infinite in possibilities.'

In other words, faith in the future, the great theme of the Victorian age of optimism, was the moving force behind the Council's creation of the QVB. Without Matthew Harris's words, which had a resounding ring of belief to them, there might have remained the suspicion, once expressed of the vast British Empire itself by one of its leading historians, that the building had been acquired 'in a fit of absent-mindedness'. The Lord Mayor further explained that 'with judicious management a marvellous centre of trade will be established here. The City Council will not be slow to formulate a policy which will attract business'. He ended on that businesslike note. The Lady Mayoress opened the Druitt Street entrance with a solid gold key presented by Edwin and Henry Phippard, the main construction contractors. The *Herald* reported that the key was 'worth more than £50' and had been made by Messrs Fairfax and Roberts. According to the *Bulletin* the gold key had been the centre of a behind-the-scenes disagreement between the Mayor and the Governor of New South Wales, Viscount Hampden.

The Governor had said that he would be happy to attend the ceremonial opening, indicating he would expect the key position in more ways than one. But Alderman Matthews believed that, since it was a municipal occasion, the Mayoral role should be central. The Governor stayed away, but 1500 other top people attended, including the Mayor of Melbourne, Alderman

The QVB in her brief hey-day with her splendid
awning, before her decline and subsequent
remodellings.

Photograph Mitchell Library.

Above: The interior festooned with streamers, flags and the Chinese paper lanterns that were a favourite of the day.
Photograph Sydney City Library.

Opposite: The QVB in 1918, about to lose her Victorian virginity.
Photograph Tyrrell Collection — ACP.

A shipment of wine bound for London leaves Lindemans, one of the early tenants of the building.
Photograph Lindemans.

McEachern. He praised the building but said he did not agree with the Council's decision to build shops within it because, as municipal property, they would be exempt from rates and thus compete unfairly with retailers elsewhere.

It seemed a sour note on a champagne occasion. But everyone else was bubbly enough and so many official guests and uninvited spectators crowded through the Druitt Street entrance into the lofty central avenue of the building that it became impossible to serve refreshments to those waiting. Sydney was so eager to see inside the QVB that there was not enough elbow room to drink the toasts.

Late in the afternoon the 600 gas lamps of the QVB were turned on for the first time. It was a magical moment. In the midwinter dusk, the great building sprang into life before the eyes of thousands of homegoing city workers and shoppers — it was a 'brilliant and dazzling' spectacle, the *Herald* reported.

That evening there was a ball and banquet at the Town Hall and the delayed toasts to the future of the QVB were drunk. Reports of the gala noted that the Lady Mayoress wore a gown of black and green velvet, that the dancing began with the Lancers, and that 'flashlight photographs were taken'. The *Herald* devoted an entire column to the names of the 1300 guests, a *Who's Who* of Sydney, although there were a few notable absentees. Governor Hampden was in Melbourne, of all places, and Lady Hampden preferred to attend a Sydney performance of *The Little Minister* at Her Majesty's Theatre. The Premier of New South Wales,

George Reid, was also absent, although for more pressing reasons. He was electioneering in the country and that evening faced a 'large and disorderly' meeting at Orange, where he was several times howled down by hecklers.

As the Lord Mayor's guests were leaving the Town Hall, they lingered on the steps to admire the midnight spectacle of the QVB, its lights still burning brightly. Almost a century was to pass before the building again enjoyed such a memorable day.

At first, though, the prospects were promising. Real estate experts advised the Council that the building could pay for itself from rents in thirty years. The cost to the Council had been £374,000 — £250,000 for construction, the rest for the part of the site purchased from the state government. Alderman Harris recognised that 'it is not to be expected that such an immense structure will immediately achieve its fullest possibilities'.

Because of its design there was less to the QVB than met the eye, at least in rentable space. Its combination of arcade, galleries and vaulted glass roofs, topped by domes, was a triumph of the visual but its viability could be questioned since more than half its space was public or decorative, leaving far less sales space than the usual retail ratio. This was the cost paid for extravagance of style. One-third of the ground floor was taken up by a central mall which quickly became known to shoppers and tenants as the Avenue, a tiled boulevard extending 190 metres between Druitt and Market streets, with thirty shops on each side. Above were two levels of galleries, each also separated by precious space.

**The grand lady loses her petticoat: demolition of the
Victorian awning in 1918.**
Photograph Council of the City of Sydney.

The strollers promenading on the Avenue could, between window shopping, look upwards through the glass, twenty metres above, to the dome at thirty-five metres.

There remained a few finishing touches. As the first QVB tenants were moving in, half-naked statues, without which any self-respecting Victorian public building would have felt quite naked, were being hoisted high above the facades of George and York streets. The six figures in white Carrara marble, three of women, were, of course, intended to be allegorical rather than erotic. Their designer, William McIntosh, a prolific young sculptor of civic statues, said that the heroic figures, twice lifesize, symbolised national unity, the arts, science, labour, justice and business. But since the statues were twenty metres above the streets and their details thus all but invisible to passers-by, their exact messages mattered less than their general decorative effect.

It is not known who posed for the Rubens-style female forms, but McIntosh's model for the muscular male figures was the famed Sydney swimmer Percy Cavill, then twenty-four and the holder of many records in Australia and England. (Modelling, as well as swimming, seemed to run in the champion's family for his father, Fred Cavill, had swum the English Channel in 1877 and soon after was asked to pose for a London sculptor making a statue of the Prince of Wales. The head was a royal likeness but Cavill senior provided the body beautiful.)

In its first decade or so the QVB had some of the atmosphere and variety of an Oriental bazaar. The tenants conducted a lively mixture of commerce, crafts and skills. There were shops, studios, offices and workrooms for some two hundred traders, dealers, artisans and even a few sellers of dreams.

The range was from tailors to taxidermists, from purveyors of Australian wine to those of Chinese tea, from flower-sellers to fortune-tellers, from spectacle-makers to corset-fitters. There were milliners, bootmakers, glovers, herbalists, feather-dressers and other caterers to the carriage trade. There was an importer of fly-catchers and a seller of rabbit netting.

There were household names like Singer and Lysaghts taking orders for substantial things like sewing machines and galvanised iron. And there were purveyors of less tangible services — Madame Leonora Leigh and Professor Davenport read palms and J.W. Tyler read minds. Mr G.B. Modini sold guns and the Christian Science reading room offered hope. In the basement, Messrs Penfolds and Lindemans had vast cellars stocking half a million bottles of wine.

Resounding company titles were much in favour. The 'sight specialist', Mr W. Randle Woods, conducted the Ocularium, Quong Tart ran the Elite tea room. The Ideal Portrait Company asked clients to watch the birdie and the School of Intelligent Piano Playing was directed, no doubt intelligently, by R.E. Vick. The Pearl-like Tooth Paste Company, the Success Publishing Corporation and the Federal Hair Pad Company announced themselves boldly.

There was a studious, scholarly air to much of the activity in the galleries. As well as housing the Public Library and

The sad facade of the QVB — her glory days over.
Photo Council of the City of Sydney.

The Druitt Street end of the building, long home to Lindemans and the Post Office, during the first remodelling.
Photograph Council of the City of Sydney.

Blanchard's bookshop, the QVB was a centre of popular culture and self-improvement. Apart from sheet-music shops, piano-sellers and piano-tuners, there were the salons of private teachers of music, dancing, singing, elocution, painting, sculpting, drawing and dressmaking. A generation of young Sydney people trooped up the stone stairs of the QVB with their music cases, ballet shoes, brushes and sewing boxes to take lessons from Professor Ernest Truman, Miss Florence Tweedle, Madame Nettie Summerville, Mr Nelson Illingworth and many other teachers of artistic and useful skills. From Miss Mann, sewing students bought the latest Parisian paper patterns.

The more decorous of sports were played there, too — there was Louis Darrell's billiards saloon, Miss Violet McKenzie's gymnasium for ladies and the Elite table tennis hall.

Religion and good works were also well represented within this temple of commerce and pleasures. Apart from the Christian Science Library, the Young Women's Christian Association, the Anglican Diocese of Sydney, the Australian Board of Missions, the Church Book Store and the Diocesan Waifs and Orphans Fund all rented rooms. The Salvation Army band played outside the Market Street entrance on Saturday evenings, interrupting, according to some complaints, the more secular music in the Concert Hall above. Some unions found the QVB a handy address, including the railwaymen, the municipal workers, and the Institute of Journalists.

There was also tragedy in the building for the most successful of its early tenants, Quong Tart, a Chinese businessman who, said the *Daily Telegraph,* was 'as well known as the Governor himself and quite as popular among all classes'. In an era of individual and official racism — the Immigration Restriction Act of 1901 included the notorious 'dictation test', a language examination designed to exclude unwanted (i.e., non-white) immigrants — Quong Tart's was a remarkable success story. He arrived from China in 1865 at the age of nine, worked first on the Araluen (NSW) goldfields, moved to Sydney, and became the best-known restaurant owner of his day. In 1896 Nat Gould, the English journalist, later famous as a racing writer, wrote of him as one of the most respected and popular citizens of Sydney. 'He has the manners of an educated European and the habits of a gentleman. He is a good employer, and a man of unbounded generosity. His wife is an Englishwoman and Mr Quong Tart sometimes poses as a Scotchman. It is an unaccustomed sight to see a Chinaman in kilts and to hear him sing a Scotch song. He dances the Highland fling with great gusto.'

By the time the QVB opened, this prosperous and picturesque figure presided over the city's most popular 'dining saloon' at 137 King Street which stayed open until 11.30 pm for the 'especial convenience' of audiences at the nearby theatres. A typical Quong Tart theatre supper was Manning River oysters, hot 'Scotch' pies, passionfruit and ice cream, apple tartlets, and 'my famous tea'. He also catered for picnics 'on the mazy paths of Mosman, the breezy heights of Bondi, and other beauty spots', to which his staff delivered baskets of 'the best of provender' but

The grand Avenue on the ground floor was totally
destroyed.

Photograph Council of the City of Sydney.

On the ground floor, the magnificent arches led only to a warren of pokey rooms.
Photograph Council of the City of Sydney.

no Chinese dishes.

Quong Tart also had tearooms in the Royal Arcade and the Sydney Arcade, and in 1899 he opened another in Room 15 of the QVB, facing George Street. This did so well that in 1902 he also rented Room 55 on the York Street side, both serving 'my special cakes and pastry'. He then took a four-year lease, at £675 a year , of Rooms 69-76 on the first floor overlooking the central avenue of the building and converted this space into the Elite, which he publicised as 'a spacious and elegant hall for banquets, balls, socials, concerts and meetings'. His daily advertisements in the newspapers were as inviting as his food — they assured readers that 'dining contentedly' at his tables they would find 'members of parliament, judges, lawyers, bankers, journalists, doctors, clergymen, merchants, and, in fact, everybody who is anybody.'

Such success attracted envy, or at least attention, for only a few months after the Elite opened a man walked into Quong Tart's office, Room 78, bashed him with an iron bar, stole £20 and escaped. A man was later convicted of the assault and sentenced to twelve years' imprisonment but Quong Tart never recovered from the attack and died a year later. His family and partners kept the Elite going until 1905, when the hall was rented as an importer's sample room.

The Quong Tart tragedy was also a sad blow to the QVB, for the Elite and the tearooms enlivened the building, and to Australia, which lost an able and generous man who was also, as historian Gavin Souter later wrote, 'the most distinguished and

best-assimilated Chinese' in the Australia of the day.

The grandeur of the building impressed visitors but it seemed to overawe some potential tenants. At least, there was no immediate rush to rent. In its first year of business the building attracted only forty-seven tenants, although there were spaces for almost two hundred. But in the following year another twenty leases were signed, including two that could generate customers for adjacent shops — a post office and a branch of the New South Wales Public Library. By 1905 there were 150 tenants, and by 1915 there were about 200.

This was steady progress, but successive City Councils were never satisfied. The QVB had found its own level, attracting a mixture of businesses that in its variety was as eccentric and individualistic as its architecture. But it did not become the great high-rent retail centre for which Council and their accountants had hoped. The Councils of the Edwardian era had inherited a Victorian legacy and they were never sure whether it was ahead of their times or behind them. Whichever it was, it did not suit them and, being at heart tinkerers rather than thinkers, they were forever snapping at the skirts of the stately building.

As the Victorian era slipped astern and appreciation of its styles dwindled, the building that its civic creators had considered noble came to be considered a nuisance by their successors. It was no way to treat a lady, but the age of architectural gallantry was over and eventually new landlords called in the wreckers, albeit in the name of remodellers.

Inside the gallery shop-fronts were brought forward, and the voids reduced in width.

Photograph Council of the City of Sydney.

The lead-light ceiling which allowed light into the shops that now occupied the entire ground floor.
Photograph Council of the City of Sydney.

Their first blows were preceded by a war of attrition, a sort of municipal water torture. By 1907 when there were about 140 tenants, the Council was complaining that the rents were about £10,000 a year less than expenses. The tenants, in turn, complained that rents were too high — small shops cost £3 to £6 a week. The Council's response was bizarre: it would invest more to create even more space. It invited architects to submit plans for remodelling the interior and raising the roof. It was prepared to spend up to £75,000 and offered a prize of £1,000 for a design that would increase rent revenues by £12,000 a year to wipe out the deficit. This harebrained scheme collapsed in 1909 when none of the fifteen proposals was judged to be a suitable solution. Those that promised enough revenues were too expensive, and those within the budget offered too little extra rent.

Councils sulked about this setback for a while, then tried again in ways which suggested they considered the building an acute burden rather than a long-term civic asset. In 1915 the Council offered the QVB as a station for the government's planned city underground railway. When that was declined, the Council tested the commercial market for a private sale. Finding no takers, it decided 'in view of the annual loss (of £9,400) and the obvious difficulty of reconstruction' to offer the Commonwealth government a swap — QVB for GPO! It was a suggestion made, surely, with more ingenuity than hope. While it was possible to imagine the QVB becoming the world's most splendiferous post office, the Council's real estate record did not recommend it as

landlord of the landmark in Martin Place. Canberra declined and later extended the GPO.

Despite its 'obvious difficulty', the Council of 1916 decided reconstruction was necessary because the building was, or so it claimed, running at an annual loss of more than £19,000. In 1914 the Council had been about to raise the rents when the Great War broke out. A mayoral minute later said, in words that might have been better chosen, that this was 'a most inopportune time' for rent increases, and so they were deferred 'until a more convenient season'. Apparently, the Council found the year 1916, the year of bloody battles on the Somme (in which 21,000 Australians were killed in two months) to be a more opportune and convenient season to return to the great homefront issue of rents and 'reconstruction'.

Some dubious arithmetic was produced in support of the Council's claims that the QVB was an intolerable burden. The basic Council figures were that in its first eighteen years the QVB had earned £277,000 in rents against £428,000 paid out for maintenance and interest on the construction loan, an annual average loss of about £8,000. This was about £160 a week, hardly an intolerable sum. But the Council claimed the true loss was more than double that — about £19,000 a year, or nearly £400 a week.

This more impressive figure was arrived at by curious accounting which said that the QVB should also have paid about £30,000 in rates in the eighteen years, and a further £167,000 in interest on the estimated value of the municipal land on which it

The remodelling gave the once expansive interior a cramped atmosphere.

Photograph Council of the City of Sydney.

Shopfronts circa 1920.
Photograph Council of the City of Sydney.

stood. In effect, the Council said it was in debt to itself, that it should have charged itself rates — a strange piece of municipal masochism — and moreover, that it should have received interest on the value of land, most of which had been given to the citizens of Sydney by the state government in 1842 and had always been used for public purposes! These phantom losses added almost £200,000 to the purported QVB debts, making a grand total of about £350,000 since 1898.

The Council was understandably sensitive about revenue and rates because taxes of all kinds were increasing to finance the war. In 1914 the federal government increased land taxes and imposed a death duty on all estates valued at more than £1000. In 1915, a federal income tax was introduced, in 1916 an entertainment tax was imposed and in 1917 a wartime profits tax was ordered. Business in Sydney and elsewhere felt overtaxed and wanted municipal rates to be reduced or held steady.

Having convinced themselves by their own rubbery figures that they were very hard done by, the councillors declared that the QVB was an 'incubus', a word the *Oxford Dictionary* defines as 'an evil spirit or nightmare'. According to the Lord Mayor of the day, Alderman R.D. Meagher, the bad dream could only be banished by 'a thoroughly comprehensive scheme of remodelling and consequent improvement'. The incubus, having allegedly cost the citizens of Sydney many thousands of pounds, including large sums the citizens did not even know were theirs, was now to be exorcised by receiving more money. Having counted imaginary losses, the Council was prepared to pay out real money to be rid of them.

But the Council's curious arithmetic had painted it into a fiscal corner. Having declared that something must be done and indeed would be done about the spectre of the QVB, which it had portrayed as a money-eating monster, the Council found that any scheme of 'improvement' that could conceivably increase rents to balance the mythical £19,000 annual loss would be too costly.

Having no answer to their £19,000 question, the councillors, like good politicians, fell back on a new set of figures. These were prepared by the city Comptroller, J. Neale Breden. In a report to the Council on 9 January 1917, he boldly tackled the phantom figures put forward by Lord Mayor Meagher in 1916 by simply ignoring them. The real QVB annual loss, he said, was £7,000 a year. It was, he said, a 'severe loss', but it wasn't £19,000. Breden calculated that an investment of £32,000 in ground-floor alterations would increase rents, wipe out the deficit and return a surplus of £2,119 a year. Mr Breden was something of an admirer of the QVB and he concluded his report with the opinion that the Council must, in effect, consider the skyline as well as the bottom line. He wrote that 'the outstanding architectural beauty' of the building and 'its aesthetic value to the city' were advantages 'that must not be discounted'. The nightmare had turned into a thing of beauty, and moreover, Mr Breden assured the Council that it would 'in no wise be impaired by the alterations'. Further, he wrote in the bottom line of his report, the alterations would

**The QVB with her modern cantilevered awning
circa 1920.**
Photograph Council of the City of Sydney.

The intricate floor tiling vanished under timber and concrete.
Photograph Council of the City of Sydney.

'secure a financial gain' to the city.

These alterations, which eventually cost more than £40,000, were undertaken to remove what the Council saw as 'inherent flaws' in what its Victorian creators considered 'an architectural triumph'. The 1916-18 debates and decisions are significant in any study of the QVB because they form a crucial watershed in the building's history. Once its Victorian virginity had been broken there was, for fifty years, little resistance to later and more drastic assaults.

The first wave of alterations destroyed the magnificent arcade. The central avenue disappeared, six of the massive granite pillars were replaced with steel stanchions, some ground-floor shops were extended across the entire width, others were divided and marble, glass and copper finishes and fittings replaced many of the Victorian stone, cedar, iron, and plaster surfaces.

The scandalous vandalism of the Avenue, whose intricate floor tile patterns vanished under concrete, provoked a furious protest by a Sydney citizen, Arthur Vogan, who thus became a pioneer of polemics about the QVB. In a letter to the Lord Mayor in October 1917 Mr Vogan complained of 'the destruction' of the 'marvellous design upon the beautiful tesselated pavement'. He blamed this on the Council — 'a debased and ignorant lot of asses placed in power by an ignorant and stupid community'. The Lord Mayor replied without comment, merely informing Mr Vogan that his views had been 'duly noted'.

In the 'remodelling', the grand stone staircase from the central foyer to the galleries survived, but the galleries themselves were widened, providing more rentable space but reducing natural light and giving the once expansive interiors a cramped atmosphere. In all, thirty shop and office spaces were added. The Concert Hall, once almost fifteen metres high, was sliced in two and became the City Library, 'pending the erection elsewhere of a permanent building'. The library was still in the QVB more than sixty years later.

Even while the first alterations were under way, the Council was tempted to do more. Tinkering with the QVB seemed to be a municipal mania. The Council invited plans for further redesigning of the upper floors and adding two more! But this costly idea was 'postponed' until the government's plans for the cross-city railway route were known — there were still hopes that a station might adjoin the QVB basement, but also fears that rail tunnels would shift the foundations. Another cloud on the horizon was talk of building a bridge across Sydney Harbour with a main city access along York Street which might entail widening the street by slicing into the QVB.

So the 1920s began with none of the Council's concerns about the QVB diminished. In 1921 a Council report said losses in the previous five years totalled £47,000. Although the basement wine cellars and main ground floor shops were on long leases, most of the gallery occupants had weekly tenancies. They were constantly hearing rumours that made them wonder how long they could or should stay.

The centre void was lost to accommodate a lift.
Photograph Council of the City of Sydney.

**A window display from the opening of David Jones'
Elizabeth Street store in 1929.**
Photograph David Jones.

In 1922 the government decided to build the Harbour
Bridge, although the role of York Street was unclear. The following
year the Council considered further alterations but shrank back
from the estimated cost of £200,000. A few weeks later the
Council received, from a Sydney businessman whom it did not
name, an offer to purchase for £325,000 — much less than the
cost twenty-five years earlier. This was rejected, as was another
anonymous offer, this time from Melbourne, to lease the building
for fifty years at a price to be negotiated.

This outside interest suggested that the building had
tantalising commercial potential which the Council was unable
to exploit fully. In 1926 it reported that the accumulated losses
since 1900 were £211,000 and in Council debates there was
increasing talk of getting private enterprise involved in managing
the building.

In 1927 it suddenly seemed as though official help was at
hand for the Council through which its QVB problem might
literally disappear. Headlines announced: 'City White Elephant
To Go'. This was the first of threats to demolish the QVB and, as
with subsequent alarms, it turned out not to be worth the paper
it was printed on.

The proposal came from Dr John Bradfield, the chief
government engineer and the dynamic and sometimes dictatorial
planner of the Harbour Bridge. He recommended that the state
government 'acquire and demolish' the QVB in order to widen
York Street as a main city approach to the bridge. But reports of the
demise of the QVB were premature. Dr Bradfield's own arithmetic
ensured the Council would reject his plan to take the building
and its debts off the Council's shoulders. Bradfield estimated the
QVB was worth £900,000, which the government would provide
and with which the Council could pay off the £700,000 costs
and debts of the building, leaving a handy surplus. This £200,000
said Bradfield, could pay the Council's share of street widening
costs on the bridge approaches. This sounded more like conjuring
than accountancy, but Bradfield was nothing if not audacious in
his drive for his beloved bridge. A little earlier he had blithely
proposed demolishing a new bank building, worth £500,000, to
widen another city approach to the bridge. The government
decided this was too costly and, in the case of the QVB, the
Council saw no profit in Bradfield's idea — particularly since it
was already paying £100,000 a year towards preliminary street
works at the city end of the bridge.

Bradfield's offer was clearly of the 'heads I win, tails you lose'
variety. Although retaining the QVB meant retaining a headache
the Council decided the pain was preferable to the suggested cure.
In 1928 the Council considered raising the rents, but a deputation
of protesting tenants won the day. Then came a spate of new or
at least revived ideas for more profitable use of the larger spaces.
The City Library would move out and part of the government's
Museum of Science and Technology would move in. The J.C.
Williamson Company offered to lease part and convert it into a
theatre. A Melbourne 'syndicate' talked of leasing the whole

Retailing was not without its style in the period as shown by the restaurant in David Jones' Elizabeth Street store.

Photograph David Jones.

Art deco arrived at the QVB in 1935 when it became the home of the Electricity Department of the City Council.

Photograph Sydney City Council.

building for ninety-nine years. The government thought of moving in some of its offices. The Council toyed with the idea of revenue from a roof garden offering dining and dancing among the domes.

None of the suggestions came to anything. In 1933 the accumulated losses were announced as £500,000. About the only proposal the perplexed Councils of the early 1930s did not make or receive was demolition or conversion for a car park — that would come later.

In the booming 1920s, Sydney had gone car-crazy. Car registrations in New South Wales, most of them in Sydney, had increased from 28,000 in 1921 to 170,000 by 1929. The phrase 'parking problem' entered civic debates. When the Depression struck in 1930, bringing unemployment as high as 40 per cent in Sydney, cars were laid up almost as quickly as workers were laid off — registrations dropped 30,000 in a year and did not regain their 1929 levels for another five years.

When economic recovery began in 1935, motoring writers were advocating construction of car parks in the city. But by then the Council had devised a new role for its problem child — the QVB, which began as a palace of gaslight, became a temple of electricity.

By 1935, the Depression was receding, employment grew, building and business revived. It might have been a time for the QVB to attract new shops and enterprises, but the City Council decided to act rather than wait. Its own Electricity Department had grown out of its offices in the Town Hall and elsewhere and

it was decided to consolidate it in the QVB. This involved radical changes of use, interior layout and style — the vast Victorian arcade had to be diminished and redecorated, reduced and reshaped for a new lease of life. The experience may have been electrifying, but was hardly illuminating or edifying.

About £125,000 was spent, with the heaviest of hands, on the changes. They involved remodelling and wrecking, a swift and clumsy process, as tasteless as it was pragmatic. Art deco was the commercial design fashion of the day and since electrical appliances, many of them shaped or decorated in the geometric art deco style were the stock-in-trade of the Electricity Department, the Victorian interior of the QVB was declared unsuitable for the promotion of all-electric homes and all-electric futures.

The shock of the new hit the QVB. It was too sturdy to change much on the outside, although a black glass and chrome steel art deco doorway, superbly designed but incongruous, was grafted on as the entrance to the Electricity Department's main showroom. The interior was soon unrecognisable. The galleries became simply floors as the apertures of the high atrium were concreted over. Above, each level was partitioned into a warren of offices. The great glass roof remained but was masked in galvanised iron, requiring, of course, artificial light twenty-four hours a day, an expensive way of advertising electricity. The large glass inner dome was removed to make way for an air-conditioning plant. Black glass, white marble and other shiny art deco cosmetics covered the external granite pillars and internal steel frame. Here

After the voids were filled in, the first floor gallery
was transformed into an office for paying electricity
bills, transactions that seemed to be handled only by
male staff.

Photograph Sydney City Council.

In the 1940s, you could win an all-electric home while supporting the war effort.
Photograph Sydney City Council.

and there the original outlines could be glimpsed or guessed at, but overall the 'remodelling' was ruthless. The contractors were Beat Brothers Limited. When they had finished, the Council leased most of the QVB to the Electricity Department which, after some haggling, agreed to pay £25,500 a year. The City Library remained, and so did the wine cellars — and perhaps some ghosts.

These drastic changes excited little public comment or criticism. They were accepted as necessary and practical. The conservation of buildings of historical or artistic importance was not a public concern. Escape from the Depression was. Just as construction of the QVB had symbolised recovery from the brief, sharp recession of the early 1890s, so its conversion in 1935 was welcomed among the signs of new enterprise after the long Depression.

The bustle of artisans, the glittering showrooms, and the new jobs within the QVB were part of the commercial revival of central Sydney from five grim years. As shoppers began to spend again, electrical appliances were promoted as essential to modern living. Most houses in Sydney had electricity for lighting by the 1920s, but gas was more common in kitchens, bathrooms and laundries. (Indeed kerosene refrigerators, wood-chip heaters and ice-chest coolers were common into the 1940s.) The QVB, whose Victorian gas lamps had all given way to electric lighting by about 1915, became in the 1930s a centre of sales campaigns with publicity slogans like, 'Be Modern — Think Electricity' and, 'Cooking the Electrical Way is the Right Way'. To cook or take

a bath, the modern way was made easier by offers of stoves, water heaters, and other 'right way' appliances for small cash deposits with five years to pay the balance.

A new Sydney generation came to know the QVB, as a place where they paid electricity bills, instalments on electrical appliances, and shopped for more. The City Library was still there and so were the basement wine cellars with their familiar aromas drifting up to the reading rooms and sometimes even penetrating the air-conditioned displays and offices of the apostles of electricity.

The Victorians, a hard-headed lot despite their self-indulgence in ornate architecture, would have admired the QVB's part in the progress so precisely measured by the statistics of the rapid growth of electricity consumption. What they would have thought of the degradation of the interior, the brutalisation by bureaucrats of a gracious legacy, cannot be estimated. But, to use Queen Victoria's own words on another matter, it does not seem likely that they would have been amused.

When the QVB was opened in 1898 the *Sydney Mail* had commented, 'We suppose that in years to come our children's children will marvel that we could have boasted of such a wonderful building, as its points are decidely much in advance of our general city requirements'. Perhaps that was the problem — the QVB was certainly wonderful, but what was it *for*? In the case of the Garden Palace, fire had intervened before it could become a monumental embarrassment. But the QVB was made of sturdier, sterner stuff.

A temple to electricity!
Photograph Sydney City Council.

If some great buildings have personalities and souls — and it is tempting to imagine or invent them — then perhaps QVB may be visualised as a Gulliver long constrained and humiliated by Lilliputians with pinstripes and balance sheets. But since the building was named for a Queen, and was long talked of in Sydney as a lady, its most appropriate persona is, unlike Gulliver, feminine. One image of the QVB has been that of the sleeping beauty — a princess waiting to awake to life. But before that happened a very different fate threatened.

In its new role the QVB did not suffer the indignity of a name change — it did not become 'Electricity House', for example. The Library, Penfold's Wines, Singer Sewing Machines and Fletcher Jones' clothing were the main private tenants, but the Sydney County Council had more than half the building and SCC were the initials most closely identified with it for the next thirty years. Part of the basement became a garage and the City Rat-Catcher managed to get himself a cubicle from which to conduct his campaigns. When war came again in 1939, some weak-nerved official ordered a warren of concrete bomb shelters built in the basement. When the war spread to the Pacific, firespotters were posted on the roof of the QVB and a hole was knocked in the southern curve of the main dome through which they peered nightly, ever alert for the Japanese blitz that never came.

After the war there was desultory Town Hall talk of the future of the QVB. It was clear that the expanding Sydney County Council would leave in a few years. By 1950 it had 300,000 customers giving it revenues which entitled it to offices more impressive than the shabby conversion at the QVB. But there was uncertainty about general city development. The office building boom of the 1960s was not then in prospect and indeed, the first major postwar commercial building rose not in the city but across the harbour — the fourteen-storey MLC building in North Sydney, completed in 1957, was then the largest office block in Australia.

In 1956-58 hotel companies, including the Hilton group, showed some interest in the QVB site. Although nothing came of their talks with the Council, it was the first time since Dr Bradfield's demolition proposal thirty years earlier that talk of the future of the QVB was predicated on replacing it.

In 1958 the SCC signed a new lease — but for a further two years only, not five. The County Council was getting itchy feet and beginning to plan the huge and hideous tower block opposite the Town Hall to which it moved its headquarters a few years later. Penfolds, which had been storing and selling wines at the QVB for more than fifty years, decided at this moment to leave. The Council had two offers from merchants willing to take over the Penfolds' space at £140 a week for ten years.

On 4 May 1959, the City Council was discussing these offers when the Lord Mayor, Alderman Harry Jensen, turned a routine meeting into one of the most dramatic moments in the long and chequered history of the QVB. He proposed that it be demolished and replaced by a civic square and an underground car park. Alderman Jensen said, 'The Queen Victoria Building site is magnificent — and the building makes inadequate use of it.' An influential voice quickly supported him — two days later a *Herald* editorial declared that on aesthetic and social grounds he had a very powerful case and urged the City Council to give the Lord Mayor's proposal the support 'it so clearly deserves'. After more than sixty years — the time between 'noble' and 'inadequate' — it seemed that the writing was on the walls and the demolisher's bells were tolling for the QVB.

Even in the 1950s, the main dome of the QVB
seemed to dominate the southern end of the city.
Photograph John Fairfax & Sons.

THE GREAT DEBATE

'The Queen Victoria Building site is a magnificent one — the building makes inadequate use of it'.
                        Alderman Harry Jensen, Lord Mayor of Sydney, 1959

'The Queen Victoria Building is a rare example of architectural style and should be preserved'.
                        J.M. Freeland, Professor of Architecture, University of New South Wales, 1960

'I feel obliged to reaffirm that the Australian ugliness is not only unique in several ways, but is also worse than most other countries' kinds'.
                        Robin Boyd, architect and critic, in 'The Australian Ugliness' first published in 1960.

'Given the more conservation-conscious climate of the eighties, the Australian architect now looks back with some dismay at the boom years of the sixties'.
                        Dr Jennifer Taylor, Associate Professor of Architecture, Sydney University, 1986

These views and voices illustrate the range of the debate on architecture and urban development which began in Australia in the 1960s, a debate which persists, at varying temperatures, in the 1980s. The start in 1959 of the struggle to save the QVB was not the opening shot in the evolution of architecture from 'the most useful art' (as Francis Greenway described it in a letter to Governor Macquarie in 1814) to a subject of controversy in Australia. The origins of the arguments, which expanded to become part of the permanent agenda of public and political issues, can be traced in part to the great dispute about the Sydney Opera House. This was a turbulent affair. Now a favourite and familiar image of Sydney, its design in 1957 by Joern Utzon set off a decade of bitter controversy about shape, cost, function, and delay which created a voracious public and media appetite for arguments about architecture.

'The most useful art' became news. Some of its practitioners emerged from the anonymity of their drawing offices to become 'personalities', with public faces and public voices. It was soon common to hear and overhear people saying they knew nothing about architecture but knew what they liked. Architectural feuds became fashionable. Compared to the spectacular brawls about the Opera House — which led to Utzon resigning from the direction of his masterwork in 1967 — the QVB argument was at first a sideshow, a quiet controversy.

Alderman Jensen's demolition proposal at first attracted more support than opposition. Letters to editors claimed the QVB was 'overdue for demolition' and that Sydney needed a traffic-free city square for civic occasions. Some saw it as an ideal site for a great fountain that would 'splash and roar' in a paved piazza. Town Hall officials bravely estimated that revenues from a car park underneath could help pay for demolition and construction of a

A bad idea whose time never came — the recurring
nightmare of total demolition of the QVB. In 1959
Lord Mayor Harry Jensen displayed one such
proposal.

Photograph John Fairfax & Sons.

The Cahill Expressway was already scarring Circular
Quay in April 1961, construction of the Opera
House was started, and the first 'glass box', the multi-
storey AMP building, was challenging the AWA
tower as a landmark of Sydney.

Photographs David Moore.

The MLC building in North Sydney had predated the AMP by three years, and achieved a similar domination.
Photograph David Moore.

square. *The Herald* said this presented 'an opportunity we should seize' on both economic and aesthetic grounds. It argued that 'Sydney has paid so little attention to aesthetics in its rapid and haphazard growth, that any opportunity to add a little beauty and dignity should be eagerly grasped.' It noted that 'increases in the value of the sites fronting the square could be expected to offset the loss of rent' from the QVB. In any case, said the *Herald*, the City Council should 'look beyond revenue returns to its overriding responsibilities to a great city'.

When Alderman Jensen suggested an international design competition — such as produced the Opera House — to plan a square, he was supported by leading architects. There were dissenting voices, however. Alderman Ernie O'Dea, a former Lord Mayor, and like Alderman Jensen a member of the ruling Labor Party group in the Council, said the QVB should be retained and sold as a retail centre. Town planners interviewed by the newspapers were all for demolition, but their ideas on a replacement varied from a pedestrian precinct to, of all things, a high-rise car park. Professor Freeland spoke up for preservation of the building, but Alderman Jensen replied that he remained 'quite firm', and because he had a majority on the Council it seemed only a matter of time before he would act. The Council devised a scheme whereby QVB rent revenues would be set aside to pay for its demolition, recalling those dictatorships which require that a condemned man's estate pays for the bullets used to execute him.

By this time, 1961, Alderman Jensen had more important political matters to occupy him. He was the Labor Party candidate for the traditionally conservative northern Sydney seat of Bennelong in the federal election of that year, and such was his prominence and popularity as Lord Mayor of Sydney that he came very close to winning. After that diversion he returned to civic affairs to find that the County Council was seeking another long lease of the QVB and estimating that it would be another three or four years before its new offices were ready.

Ironically, the County Council, which had done most to diminish the QVB, thus became the key obstacle to its demolition and the agent of a reprieve. The City Council could hardly evict the County Council. It renewed the lease for a maximum of five years — in effect a stay of execution but not yet a full pardon for the QVB. The *Herald*, taking the long view, said a new civic square on the site was still possible.

Although demolition was postponed, decay was inevitable because the city spent little on exterior maintenance. One result was that in 1963 the Council had to pay £2,600 to a contractor to remove the sixty-eight decorative copper turrets dotted about the roof between the domes. The turrets, each 1.5 metres high, were beginning to shake dangerously in high winds. The contractor took them away as part of the job, and they were scattered into Sydney homes as souvenirs and pot-plant holders. (In 1977 one was found in a garden in the Sydney suburb of Birchgrove and sold at auction for $400.) The sight of workmen taking away bits of the building stimulated its admirers, who had been reassured by the

During the 1960s, all eyes were on Bennelong Point.

Photograph David Moore.

reprieve, into reviving the question of its future.

They were also stirred to speak out by the start of construction in February 1965 of a twenty-eight-storey office tower for the County Council. Once that was finished the QVB would lose its main tenant and perhaps its last chance of survival.

As the QVB debate picked up steam, the advocates of preservation and restoration were the most vocal, but they did not have the stage to themselves and even the defenders of the QVB differed about uses for the building. One of the first architects to enter the debate was Elias Duek-Cohen, who challenged the *Herald's* description of the building as 'hideous'. (This description was a case of the pot calling the kettle black. *The Herald,* which had once occupied a dignified building in Hunter Street, had moved to an office near Broadway which was almost certainly the ugliest commercial structure erected in Sydney in the 1950s.) In a 1965 letter to the paper he admitted that the neglected building had become 'inefficient, uncomfortable, and depressing', but, he wrote, 'It has a fine facade in warm-coloured stone and with columns and mouldings forming a richly-modelled surface.' Moreover, he wrote, 'it also has the only dome of any size in Sydney and creates a lively and interesting skyline. It only needs to be remodelled internally to be a very satisfactory building.' Mr Duek-Cohen did not oppose the idea of a new city square, but said the QVB site was thoroughly unsuitable since its long, narrow shape would result in one 'of uncomfortable proportions, likely to end up as an island surrounded by streams of traffic'. He claimed that 'a far more satisfactory square could be created by pulling down the untidy assortment' of commercial structures opposite the QVB in George Street.

Norman Edwards, a lecturer at Sydney University, also warned that the QVB site would not work as a plaza, 'being in the wrong place, on the edge of the city centre, and bordered by heavy traffic'. Apart from that, the QVB merited preservation for its own sake — 'it is architecturally more successful than most buildings in Sydney. Its form is strongly sculpturesque — sorely needed in an age of sterile boxes. The domes have a wonderfully exuberant quality . . . the original fine arcaded and domed

interior space has been abused but could be restored . . . the QVB instead of dying could gain a new lease of life.'

These statements of support from architects led to letters to editors complaining about the style of Sydney's spate of 'glass box' buildings, and comparing them unfavourably with the QVB. One letter to the *Herald* praised the QVB as 'an attractive, even romantic, ornament to the city, a unique asset when Sydney is looking more and more like Dallas'. Another correspondent said it would be 'criminal' to demolish 'an attractive link with the past which is a delightful contrast to the glass skyscrapers we see spiking into the sky all over Sydney'. In similar vein was a letter in several Sydney newspapers from a citizen saying demolition would be a 'crime' because Sydney 'is losing more and more of its real character' to the advance of 'enormous glass boxes'. At least some of the support for retaining the QVB, whatever its future role, arose from distaste for the stark, multi-storey, curtain-wall towers springing up in Sydney's unplanned and uncontrolled office building boom in the 1960s. The landmarks, the steel and glass exclamation marks, of this revolution included the twenty-one-storey AMP tower (1961), twenty-two-floor federal government offices in Chifley Square (1963), the twenty-seven-floor Water Board building (1965), the thirty-eight-floor state government office block (1967), and the circular fifty-floor Australia Square (1968).

To throw up new buildings, developers tore down old ones, replacing stone with glass and concrete. Demolition, excavation and construction never stopped. A new joke about Sydney was coined in this decade of craters and cranes. A visitor, asked for an opinion of the city, replies; 'It will be a nice place when it's finished.'

In 1961-64 the amount of floor space added to the city was double the additions of the previous three years. And in the next three years there was another 50 per cent increase. In all, twelve million square feet (1.1 million square metres) of commercial space was added to the centre of Sydney in the 1960s. The Sydney architect and historian Dr Jennifer Taylor has written that 'Sydney suffered the most and absorbed the highest benefits' from the 1960s building boom and its 'rapacious development', and in the late

1960s Sydney looked as if it were recovering from bomb damage — with large craters scarring the sites, hoardings marking the streets, and cranes puncturing the skyline.

The same image of bomb damage was also used by the Sydney writer Leo Schofield in recalling the architects' assault on Sydney in the mid-1960s. In 1986 he wrote, 'When I returned in 1965 I was appalled at the wholesale destruction . . . ah, Sydney, how beautiful you were before those piranha developers moved in and made a serious attempt to recreate downtown Frankfurt in the South Pacific . . . the developers were trying to prove that they could do as good a job on Sydney as the Allied bombers had done on Dresden . . .'

This 'Manhattan-on-the-Pacific' development as the social historian Peter Spearritt described the eruption of skyscrapers overlooking the harbour, was ironically helpful to the cause of the QVB. For many citizens — 'a vast number', according to one *Herald* letter — the shock of the new inspired affection for the old. Alarmed by the spectacular changes to the Sydney cityscape between the Town Hall and Circular Quay, they sought comfort in the familiar forms of Victorian architecture, perfectly expressed by the QVB.

Overall, however, the new towers were popular, admired as proofs of modernity and progress. The developers who profited, the architects who designed them, the workers who built them and office staffs who enjoyed their air conditioning and views all agreed that they were not only bigger but better. In the 1968 edition of *The Lucky Country*, the critic Donald Horne commented, 'Some of the new buildings that are going up all over Sydney and Melbourne are not bad; at least there is somewhat more unity and style in their glittering glass than in the nondescript Victorian buildings that have been knocked down. There are few grand visions, although in Sydney one can detect the beginnings of dreams of architectural grandeur.' By Mr Horne's stern standards, that was praise indeed. Significantly, in the first edition of his celebrated book in 1964, he had not mentioned the arrival of the first truly tall buildings. Four years later he added comment on them, an indication that they had quickly made a mark and earned

a place in social history.

The high-rise fever infected Alderman John Armstrong. When he became Lord Mayor in 1965, he envisioned not a city square on the QVB site but a 'multi-storey development'. But a few months later his proposal was abandoned as over-ambitious for a Labor City Council whose future was uncertain under the conservative state government elected in 1965.

In any case, the County Council would not be ready to leave the QVB for several more years. Before then, there would be time to decide what to do, or so it seemed. But then fate, in the form of politics, intervened to the benefit of the QVB. In 1967 the Liberal Party government, enjoying power and flexing its political muscle after a generation out of office, sacked the City Council. Since the Council was controlled by the Labor Party, its dismissal was seen as based as much on party politics as on claims that the Council had been corrupt and incompetent.

The Council was replaced by a committee of commissioners, bureaucrats given powers of administration but not of policy. This meant that until elected municipal government resumed, there could be no decision on the QVB. This gave its admirers another opportunity to campaign. In 1967, with the County Council's new offices rising fast above George Street and due for occupation within a year, the National Trust (NSW), in its first intervention in the debate, declared that the QVB should be saved because of its historical importance. The Trust listed the building in its 'B' category ('recommended for preservation') and described it as a 'visual asset' to the city. A voice from the building's first days also spoke in its defence — as a fourteen-year-old draughtsman, Mr Rex Shaw had helped prepare the working drawings for the stonemasons making the exterior decorative friezes. At eighty-three, he recalled what he described as 'my biggest job' — the drawings were in sections each fifteen metres long — and hoped it could be saved. Young Sydney architects joined the campaign, praising the QVB's 'visual imagery' and its 'opulent Victoriana'. They said that with $4 million and eighteen months' restoration work, the QVB — which the *Herald* was then describing as looking 'a dreary mess' — could be brought to life again and made

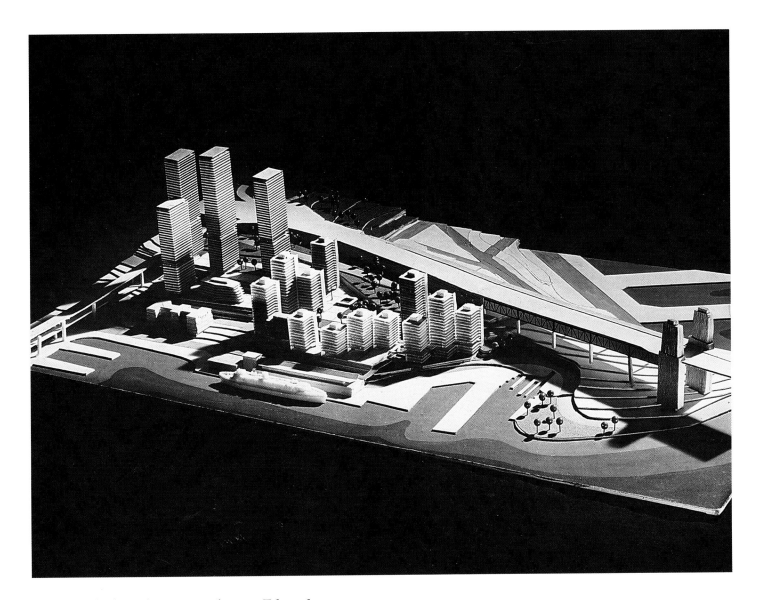

What might have been — architects Edwards
Madigan and Torzillo's prize-winning scheme for
redevelopment of the Rocks. It seemed sensible to
the government to clear the old hotels and workers'
cottages and commercially exploit the area.

Photograph Laurence Le Guay & John Nisbett.

economically viable. The group proposed 'stripping away the disfigurements', restoring the glass vault roof, ground floor arcades, tiled floors, and stone stairs, and linking the building by a shopping tunnel to the Town Hall railway station. The main dome, they suggested, could become a planetarium, with the upper gallery floors used for an art gallery, library and restaurants. These suggestions attracted approving letters to newspapers hailing the QVB as an 'architectural treasure' and calling for its preservation 'to protect what little is left of early Sydney' and as 'a reminder of some part of our short history'. Aesthetics, nostalgia and sentiment were emphasised, but no hard-headed economic solution was in prospect. The City Commissioners decided, however, that, while the QVB's future was outside their mandate, they would spend $100,000 to renovate the City Library. By now this was scattered and shabby, occupying bits and pieces on four levels of the QVB's contorted innards. But apart from these makeshift measures, the Commissioners said they would leave the decision to the politicians when they returned to the Town Hall. The Civic Reform Association, the non-Labor group in municipal politics, sensed that the QVB, or the more general debate of development versus preservation, would be an issue whenever the election was held. It said that its policy was that buildings of historic value should be preserved and restored. Did the QVB qualify? On that, 'the public should be heard before a Council decision'. In other words, Civic Reform, which was favoured to win the election, was willing to be guided by the continuing debate. So the decade

of the demolisher and developer was ending with Sydney showing the scars and the successes of their work — and with growing public concern for what had been and might be lost in the rush of change.

One sign of this was an exhibition by senior architecture students of the University of New South Wales of four plans for the future of the QVB. Visitors were asked to write comments and seventy-eight did so. Of these, sixty-five commended a plan for complete restoration. The other schemes were for shortening the building by demolishing the southern end, retaining only the main dome and central foyer and surrounding the rump with a plaza and total demolition to make way for gardens and a library. A *Herald* columnist commented that this support for restoration was a 'rebellion against the architecture of Sydney today and its matchboxes of steel, concrete and glass'. The writer said the response showed 'a conscience about depriving future generations of relics of the past'. Nevertheless, John Armstrong, the former Lord Mayor who was the Labor Party candidate for the next mayoral elections, said late in 1969 that if elected he would propose demolition of the QVB, which he said was a 'firetrap', to make way for a civic square.

A few months later the National Trust gave the QVB a new classification, 'A', which defined it as 'urgently in need of acquisition and preservation'.

The Trust also convened a public meeting attended by 160 partisans of the QVB. They were startled by one of the first speakers, George Molnar, who taught architecture at Sydney University

The Victoria Arcade *(opposite)* **with its superb elliptical glass dome and the Royal Arcade** *(left)* **were demolished. By the 1970s, only the Strand Arcade and the shell of the QVB remained.**
Photographs Mitchell Library.

and for many years had drawn for the *Herald* cartoons variously viewed as reactionary, cynical or urbane. Professor Molnar said he considered the building 'ugly'. However, he said, it had 'a beautiful dome' and it should be saved 'because whatever replaced it would be even uglier'. Molnar's comments and previous defences of the QVB by teachers of architecture illustrated one of the divisions in the 1960s debate over the rebuilding of Sydney: that between many 'academic' and many 'commercial' architects. Elias Duek-Cohen, an early opponent of demolition, told the meeting that the QVB should be preserved because of 'the interest it gives to a skyline increasingly dominated by "boxes"'. The meeting resolved to continue campaigning for preservation. But there was still no credible economic proposal of what to do with the building if it was saved from the wreckers.

Scores of ideas were floated in the 1960s by architects, politicians, journalists and in letters to newspaper editors. Most emphasised cultural and social uses — art galleries, museums, exhibition and musical venues, theatres, meeting halls, libraries, restaurants, cafes, a flower market, a planetarium and so on.

But Sydney had theatres, museums, and libraries, it was building an opera house and, in any case, everybody knew that culture was costly and had to be subsidised. Every time politicians and bureaucrats heard the word 'culture' they feared they might have to reach for the public cheque book — except in the case of construction of the Opera House which had a virtual blank cheque from the State Lottery.

In 1971 the Royal Australian Institute of Architects (NSW chapter) added its prestigious voice to the preservation campaign on the grounds of the QVB's historical importance. The Institute said 'new functions' could be found for the QVB but it did not define them.

What was clear, however, by 1971 was that there would be some sort of future for the QVB, although what its role would be was far from clear. The rumours of rescue finally became reality when the new Lord Mayor, Alderman Emmet McDermott, leader of the Civic Reform Group, announced on 31 May that the QVB would be 'preserved and restored to its original state'. Alderman McDermott said, 'I think this is a decision that the people have been awaiting for years — this is a true interpretation of what the people want'. Certainly it was what the admirers of the QVB had long sought and fought for. The National Trust praised the decision as reflecting 'great credit' on the Civic Reform Group and recalled that only three years earlier 'there were reasons to have serious doubts whether the building had much future'.

The Lord Mayor's announcement, which he described as 'a gift to the city by the Council', came as a surprise, at least in its timing. In its election policy, Civic Reform had made clear its concern to 'preserve buildings of historic value', but its decision on the QVB had been expected to be revealed some months later when the Council was due to reveal a 'strategic plan' for Sydney and its architectural environment. The Lord Mayor's decision also caused some political confusion. Labor members of the Council

The Royal Arcade was among the last to go. Its echoes of Florence or Rome, with its glimpses of the main dome of the QVB, made way for the undistinguished Hilton Hotel.

Photographs David Moore.

opposed preservation of the QVB, but the Federal Labor Party spokesman on urban affairs, Tom Uren MP, said a Labor government would assist Councils to restore historic buildings, and that the QVB would have high priority.

Among those surprised but unfazed by the timing of the rescue of the QVB was the writer-actor Barry Humphries, an ardent admirer of Victorian architecture. At the moment the Lord Mayor announced the good news, Mr Humphries was lecturing university students on the virtues of preserving the best of old buildings. He included a special plea for the QVB in the form of these verses, not the smoothest of his writings but certainly sharp-tongued.

Your domes dream of Constantinople;
Facade picturesque;
Stained glass that once glowed like an opal.
Sydney Romanesque.

They built you way back in the Boom Time,
The opulent era;
But now in the Seventies' Doom Time.
The Wrecker steals nearer.

The noose of 'Progress' slowly throttles
The old and the brave,
New towers rise like giant jumbo bottles
Of cheap after shave.

How we hate all that sandstone as golden
As obsolete guineas,
With nowhere to stable our Holden,
Or tether our Minis.

A car park, a bank or urinal
Would grace such a site;
The end could be painless and final,
The deed done by night.

Reactionary ratbags won't budge us,
Nor sentiment sway;
But how will posterity judge us,
Ten years from today?

Next day Mr Humphries' poem, as well as the Lord Mayor's announcement, was news. Humphries quickly added, for publication, a more optimistic final verse.

They've reprieved you with wisdom and vision,
A brave, solemn pledge
Let us pray that this mayoral decision's
The thin end of the wedge.

In the event, it was to be more than 'ten years from today' before the QVB's reprieve, the act of 'wisdom and vision', was crowned with restoration.

SEARCH FOR A SOLUTION

AFTER a decade of debate, the 1971 decision to preserve and restore the QVB was not the end of the saga. Rather, it was the start of the search for a solution to architectural and financial problems which, like the building itself, were large and complex. They involved politicians, civic administrators, planners, architects, developers, and financiers who faced a basic question: how to restore the QVB to its former visual glory and still ensure its viable long-term economic future. The question could be stated simply enough. To answer it would require another decade of intense discussion, hard decisions and not a little daring.

There were arguments — sometimes they seemed endless — about the extent of the restoration to be attempted and what purposes the revived QVB should or could serve. But there was agreement from the start that no restoration of a Victorian building on such a scale had ever been contemplated before in Australia or elsewhere. That much was common ground about an uncommon, indeed unique project. While the project was struggling to find sponsors and momentum, there were in the Sydney of the 1970s a series of developments in architecture, construction and public opinion that sometimes helped and sometimes hindered the search for an end to the QVB problem.

There was another office building boom and a bust. There was the eruption of the 'green bans', a uniquely Australian expression of opposition to the excesses of 'developers'. There were radical changes in municipal, state, and federal governments. More Sydney landmark buildings were lost, some were saved and new ones rose to record heights. The face of the city continued to change, often for the worse, sometimes for the better.

It was a turbulent decade in Sydney. During those years it gradually became evident — and more details have emerged since — that Sydney was beset by political and police corruption, organised crime, narcotics trafficking, and taxation rackets.

It was a period in which the media, business, and government decided that Sydney was taking on an 'international' atmosphere, whatever that meant apart from such multinational symbols as high-rise buildings and fast food. Certainly, the tall headlines about low life in high places had a Chicagoesque flavour, but that was no novelty for Sydneysiders with good memories or some interest in local history. John Norton, the muckraking editor of the 1890s, would have felt at home among the Sydney hustlers of the 1970s.

However, despite or because of the ruthless pursuit of profits by some players in the city 'development' lottery, concern for Sydney's architectural heritage and its physical future took on new and vigorous life. It began among vocal minorities but soon became part of mainstream politics.

One, but not the first, of the major signals and symbols of this change, which persists in the 1980s, was the opening of the Opera House in 1973. After sixteen years of controversy and construction and a cost of $100 million, the spectacular structure, which the Australian writer Clive James wryly described as looking like a 'portable typewriter full of oyster shells' was ready. It passed

A Public Meeting to establish the Friends of the Queen Victoria Building

**6.30pm Monday
18th February 1980
at the building**

*through the George St entrance
2nd Floor*

Join by sending $10 to "the Friends" at P.O. Box Q160 Queen Victoria Building N.S.W. 2000

The QVB has had her friends and defenders since
the turn of the century, but it took the challenge of
restoration to drive them to public meetings.
City of Sydney Public Library.

The grand interior of the building was reduced to a series of numbingly tedious offices, and the exterior defaced by discount advertising.
Photograph David Moore.

from its architects, engineers and artisans to artists and administrators. The formal opening, by Queen Elizabeth, ignited a warm outer glow of Sydney civic pride. It also stimulated popular appreciation of the social, cultural and economic values of great buildings. This usefully reinforced the wider concern for the quality of city life which manifested itself as the urban environment movement.

In Sydney in 1971 a stretch of bushland, known as Kelly's Bush, was threatened with destruction by dense residential development. The local residents protested in vain to the builders and local and state authorites.

They had the inspired idea of asking the Builders Labourers' Federation (BLF) for help. Surprised by the approach from residents of a conservative, affluent suburb, the left-wing union decided the cause deserved support and warned the builder that if it touched Kelly's Bush, workers would retaliate against all the company's Sydney projects by indefinite strikes. The company retreated and Kelly's Bush was saved.

A BLF member commented 'This was not a black ban, but a green ban', and the phrase passed into the Australian language. The *National Times* described the BLF members as 'Sydney's social conscience'. And the *Guardian* of London said the union's New South Wales secretary, Jack Mundey, a Communist, could be called 'Australia's most effective conservationist'. The *Guardian* added 'Middle-class groups are a little embarrassed at having to turn to a rough-hewn proletarian Communist to protect them from

developers, but approach him they do . . .'.

The Premier of New South Wales, Robin Askin, denounced these tactics as 'proletarian planning', but it was clear that selective use of the green bans had much public support. In 1972 environmental strike threats were used to protect the Botanic Gardens and Centennial Park, Sydney's most important green spaces. Askin's *laissez-faire* government was the loser on each occasion.

The 'green bans', which had an attractive simplicity and rare 'power to the people' appeal, were dramatic evidence that the era of environmentalism had arrived. In the New South Wales municipal elections in 1971, conservation and environmental issues showed up in campaigning and voting. In 1971 the Faculty of Architecture at Sydney University offered its first course in conservation of old buildings. In 1972, 'quality of urban life' issues were important in the election, for the first time in twenty-three years, of a Federal Labor government — which then legislated for urban improvement and heritage protection. Jack Mundey, who was later expelled from his union in a factional dispute, recalls that 1971-72 were years of 'total confrontation with the developers', but that in 1973-74 the developers usually sought union or residents' opinions before planning or building. A history of the BLF, entitled *Taming the Concrete Jungle* says the forty green bans in 1971-73 halted, amended, or delayed construction projects with a face value of $3 billion.

The green bans attracted international attention but no

direct emulation overseas. The American sociologist, Richard J. Roddewig, in his 1978 history of the bans, says they numbered forty-three in 1971-74 and affected projects with an estimated value of $4 billion. One-quarter of the bans involved preservation of historic buildings or areas. Another quarter involved inner-city housing disputes between high-rise schemes and low-income residents, particularly in the Rocks area and Woolloomooloo.

Richard Roddewig concluded that the green ban movement had 'worldwide significance', and showed 'the refusal of workers to build socially or environmentally destructive projects'. That was overstating the case, as events have proved since. But the comment indicated the wide interest in the green bans and reflected hopes that they could have lasting impact and imitators. Indeed, the green bans were significant. But perhaps their statistics, although impressive, were less important than their crucial role in raising public consciousness about the state of the cities.

The green bans worked well enough to make developers somewhat more careful and more conscious of the environment. To some extent the green bans receded because of the recession in city construction in Sydney in the mid-1970s. Three major developers, overextended in an overbuilt market, went bankrupt and others shelved plans and retrenched workers. Political changes in the construction unions and economic pressures on their members made bans, of any colour, impractical for the rest of the 1970s.

In retrospect the green bans, although sincere and even idealistic, might appear as a luxury which the BLF and other construction workers could afford while they had plenty of work. But influential economic groups, unions among them, rarely use their muscle for wider good, even when they can afford to. Thus the unique contribution of the building workers' green bans have a red-letter place in the history of the defence of Sydney's environment.

The green bans helped to dramatise and moderate what was fast becoming an urban crisis. In 1972 Peter Keys, a councillor of the Royal Australian Institute of Architects, had declared that every building of historic importance in Australia was in danger because state and local governments had no powers to prevent owners demolishing their properties. He added, 'Of course, the cost of preservation must be weighed against the need for continued economic growth — but it seems that the powers-that-be think economic progress and growth are related to demolition and erecting multi-storey buildings'. The Sydney architect Norman Edwards took up this theme in an article in the National Times, charging that 'progress is being defined as newness for its own sake, and the consequence of this, environmentally, is bushland bulldozed . . . and fine old buildings ripped up . . .' In its Strategic Plan of 1971, the Sydney City Council had pointed to the dangers, and one of the Plan's objectives was to 'conserve, enhance, and improve the physical environment of the city'. The Plan, which emphasised attainable goals rather than unenforceable restrictions, warned 'The history of Sydney is unique — and its old buildings, precincts, structures, and details are the physical expressions of this history . . . an invaluable part of the city is being destroyed through redevelopment and there is a real danger that Sydney will become a 'faceless' city because the new buildings are more and more international in style and homogeneous in appearance . . . economic pressure for redevelopment is strong and economic incentives for preservation are weak . . .'.

At the same time, a UNESCO report on urban conservation noted, 'A city without old buildings is like a person without a memory'. As the Sydney architecture teacher Jennifer Taylor said later, 'a city remembers itself through its old buildings'. Put another way, thoughtless demolition is civic lobotomy.

In 1973 the new federal government ordered a register of the National Estate to be made, listing the nation's natural and built heritage. The words 'environment', 'conservation', and 'heritage' entered political vocabularies. As the uproar around the green bans began to subside, another environmental battle broke out on a very different front — Fraser Island, the largest sand island in the world. An American company, apparently with no thought for the island's unique, fragile and wind-sculpted structure, proposed bulldozing its dunes and beaches to extract minerals. The ultra-conservative and anti-conservationist Queensland government gave permission, touching off a long and bitter battle.

The marvellous stained glass window overlooking
York Street served merely as a backdrop to the most
mundane of offices.
Photograph David Moore.

Fluorescent lights hung untidily from the ceiling of the Concert Hall and mocked its Victorian opulence.
Photograph David Moore.

The island was eventually saved by Canberra government interventions in 1975-76.

Meanwhile, back at the QVB, these were slow rather than stirring times. Nothing much was happening inside where only the city librarians, Council clerks, and a dozen short-lease retailers remained, all feeling rather lonely in the shabby shell. Outside, wheels were grinding slowly towards decisions.

In 1974 the National Trust, the independent pressure group dedicated to conserving historic buildings and natural beauty, upgraded the QVB to its top drawer, top priority 'classified' list. This defined its preservation as 'essential to the nation's heritage'. It was like giving the QVB a Victoria Cross, a PhD and a Nobel Prize all in one. The Trust described the building as 'a superb example of High Victorian architecture' which, with its neighbours, the Town Hall and St Andrew's Cathedral, 'forms a visually exciting group of buildings'.

The City Council had other measures of the QVB's worth. Whereas the Council of 1959, bent on demolition, had given it a notional value of $1 million, the Council of 1974 estimated its value at $30 million and proposed to spend $4 million on restoration. The Council invited anyone interested to search attics and archives for material to guide authenticity in restoration. One valuable result was that a niece of the QVB architect George McRae donated an album of photographs, including illustrations of the interiors. This was a happy and fitting gesture: a link to the building's creator helpful to its recreators.

No program or target date for restoration had been set and in 1976 serious doubts arose about timing and cost. It was pointed out that restoration of Elizabeth Bay House, a rundown Regency mansion dating from 1837, had cost $750,000, far more than estimated. And the conservative federal government, which had succeeded the Labor administration dismissed in 1975, had cut all grants for National Estate purposes. The Deputy Lord Mayor, Alderman Andrew Briger, said the Council could not itself afford restoration. In effect, restoration would be delayed indefinitely, or at least until public or private funds could be found. But Alderman Briger emphasised that the Council still recognised what he called the 'national significance' of the QVB. He said, 'It is the best example of Victoriana in Australia. It is a truly magnificent building — although the interior was absolutely vandalised earlier this century. But that was the age of vandalism — it happened all over the world'.

This enthusiasm for the QVB, which was echoed in a poll of National Trust members who voted it their favourite historic building in New South Wales, led the Council to devise ways of obtaining restoration and renewal plans at minimal cost against the day when public or private funds might be available to do the work.

A 'QVB panel' of four Council officers was set up. They suggested the Council call for feasibility studies. This was a way of getting some basic thinking and planning done at no cost to the Council. The response showed there was no shortage of suitors for the hand of 'the old lady of George Street' as the popular press had taken to calling the Victorian building. No fewer than fifty-five plans and proposals were submitted in 1977. From these, the panel invited ten individuals and groups to give more details. Eight accepted and the panel whittled these down to five. They were offered a $5000 fee to produce detailed plans and models for public scrutiny. These were exhibited at the Town Hall in August 1978 and attracted 7000 visitors. Architects involved were Stephenson & Turner, Kahn Finch and Partners, and Peddle, Thorp and Walker who submitted two designs. Kell & Rigby, builders, were also involved.

The Council's QVB panel reserved comment, but the National Trust quickly sought to influence Council decisions. The Trust declared that the only design it could support was the proposal by Stephenson & Turner for full restoration to what the Trust saw as the 'original concept'. The Trust said it found the other proposals 'unacceptable'. The uses they suggested included a 400-room hotel, a 260-apartment complex and multi-purpose commercial and entertainment centres. The Trust said that alterations which would 'disrupt' or 'degrade' the 'dramatic' interior would be an 'unacceptable assault on this essential part of our heritage'.

The QVB became known to a generation of Sydney people for $2 art prints. 'Incredible Value!'
Photograph David Moore.

While the Council was wondering what next to do with the five plans, the New South Wales chapter of the Royal Australian Institute of Architects added its voice to the campaign for restoration. In a letter to Sydney newspapers, it stated, 'It is pleasing to see that the debate over the QVB is not about its demolition but about how it should be reinstated, inside and out, in the most authentic and compatible manner possible'. The RAIA, in clear criticism of the 'modernisation' aspects of some renewal proposals, said the QVB 'is no place for space-age architectural virtuosity'. It added, 'Uses must be chosen that capitalise on its architectural merit and, at the very least, are compatible with the magnificent original arcaded and galleried interior conception'.

This influential sermon from the architectual establishment went on, 'Essential new lifts, stairs, ducts and pipes must be discreetly tucked away. The real effort should be made in appreciating and accurately reinstating the rich old detailing. The restored interior is potentially a major architectural identity to be listed with landmarks such as Martin Place, Australia Square and the Opera House as contributing towards the individual character of the City of Sydney'. It was a landmark letter in the architectural debate, but it did not move the economic obstacles that remained. Indeed, the letter's final point was perhaps rhetorical rather than useful. It said that the architectural 'significance' of restoring the QVB 'should override any consideration of extracting the maximum economic return from

the site. It would bring financial as well as cultural benefits to the city'. But with estimates of restoration costs running from $9 million to $17 million, economic returns had their own significance.

A few days later, the Council decided to explore a range of economic solutions by inviting the potential restorers and renovators to back their blueprints with bank cheques. On 30 November 1978, the Council announced that the five left in the field would be asked to submit preliminary restoration and management contracts — and a $200,000 deposit as proof of their seriousness. The Council guidelines said that the interior uses of the revived building should be financially self-supporting and that the whole should, in the words of Town Clerk Leon Carter, generate its own 'life, interest and activity'.

The Town Clerk noted that the QVB had been the subject of more petitions and suggestions than any other structure in Sydney. The *Herald,* welcoming an end to 'a saga of indecision', said, 'The people of Sydney have shown that they like the building and want it to remain on its commanding site. That argument has been won. The vital question now is what should be the manner of the restoration'. It warned against turning it into 'an expensive mausoleum', rather, it 'should be restored so that it becomes a magnet for people and, as such, able to support itself'.

Commercial success, rather than the details of restoration, remained the 'vital question'. How difficult it was to solve was shown when three months later the Council rejected the five

The cold winds of change were beginning to blow through the sterile corridors of an architect-designed glass-box Sydney. The romance of the QVB, its sculpturesque and exuberant quality were coming to be seen by the population as very valuable indeed.
Photograph David Moore.

'Demolition, excavation and construction was non-stop... a visitor, asked for an opinion of the city, replies: "It will be a nice place when it is finished".'
Photograph David Moore.

detailed proposals it had invited because none of them was financially satisfactory. They either lacked investor support, promised too little revenue or required contributions or conditions the Council could not afford.

The Council's rejection of the five schemes on economic grounds seemed to consign the QVB to the 'too hard' basket. Once more the building was in a limbo between the claims of conservation and commerce. There was some talk by both the ruling Civic Reform Group on the Council and the Labor Party minority of conversion to a hotel-cum-casino. This rated a few headlines and provided a political opportunity for the state government to step into the QVB debate for the first time since its election in 1976. The energetic Minister for Environment, Paul Landa, warned the Council that the government would not allow any development that harmed the architecture. 'We insist that the historical and architectural importance be preserved', he said. Mr Landa said that the Heritage Council had the powers to prevent any alteration or demolition which it did not approve. The New South Wales Heritage Council, which some developers called 'the big green stick' was established in 1977, soon after the Labor government took office, as a conservation watchdog for the state. The Council's federal counterpart, the Heritage Commission, also registered its interest in the QVB by listing it in its highest category as a building of 'aesthetic and social significance for future generations as well for the present community'.

At the end of 1979 the Council once more decided to seek a commercial saviour for the declining building, and made it clear it would be the last attempt, the last chance.

The Council, which was paying $500,000 a year for basic maintenance, said it would not contribute to restoration costs. Town Clerk Carter put it plainly: 'The cost will not fall on the blistered shoulders of the weary ratepayer'. It wasn't exactly an ultimatum but it had an ominous tone. The Council decided to call for worldwide tenders from companies willing to lease the building and pay all the expenses of restoration, then estimated at $20 million. Mr Carter warned, 'If a suitable offer is not made the building will lie dormant for a decade or so, falling gradually into disrepair and, eventually, there will be calls for the "eye-sore" to be removed. If we can't find a wealthy visionary to preserve the building through a sound commercial base it may well be demolished eventually'.

As the search for a 'wealthy visionary' began, the *Herald* commented that although 'there is no doubt that public opinion favours preservation and revitalisation' it would be unrealistic to expect the state or federal governments to come to the rescue with public funds. 'The only remaining hope lies with private enterprise — if the building is to survive it must be made commercially viable'. Failing that, 'the future of the building looks bleak'.

Thus the decade that had begun with demolition ruled out and preservation made the policy and the priority was ending with the fate of the QVB still hanging in the balance. This alarmed many of the building's admirers. They approved the Council's

Surprisingly, some of the building was not altered.
The gentlemen's toilets with their cast-iron urinals
remained un-remodelled.

Photograph David Moore.

stipulation of 'full restoration' in the leasing invitations but decided that a monitoring and publicity group was needed during the process of choosing a developer to take a long lease on the QVB. The result was the foundation in February 1980 of the Friends of the Queen Victoria Building, with Dr Virginia Spate, Professor of Fine Arts at Sydney University, as president. The main aims of the Friends, stated in a newsletter a few weeks later, were 'to help ensure that the restoration gives full recognition to its architectural quality' and to 'encourage a broad spectrum of users' in the restored building. Put another way, the Friends intended to be watchdogs. Their committee included architects, lawyers, a merchant banker, a town planner, several businessmen and one of the few remaining QVB tenants, Mr Sam Terley, who had a menswear shop at the corner of George and Market streets.

How influential the Friends were is difficult to estimate, but they were listened to and in May 1980 the committee was invited by the City Council to examine the responses to the worldwide advertising of the restoration project.

More than twenty companies had written seeking details but the result was an anticlimax — there were only three formal tenders. A London company proposed an entertainment and restaurant centre. A Filipino company suggested a hotel and retailing complex. A Singapore group envisaged a hotel and conference rooms — this plan had, at least, the virtue of brevity in that it consisted of a single sheet of paper. None of the submissions complied with the Council's standards of restoration and all proposed alterations, partial demolition of interiors, and unacceptable financial and leasing concessions. One of the proposals described the Council's restoration requirements as 'most difficult', but in a last-ditch effort to get improved plans, the Council offered the three groups two more months in which to go back to their drawing boards and bankers.

At this stage the Friends of the QVB issued a gloomy newsletter, expressing disappointment with the offers, declaring that the Council should accept none of them, and warning of its opposition.

There then occurred one of those dramatic twists of fate and fortune that enliven the history of the QVB. Two factors were involved and they were brought fruitfully together by chance rather than intent. The first factor was a plan to restore the building, the second was a man, in fact the 'wealthy visionary' whom Leon Carter had defined as essential to solving the QVB conundrum. The plan in its first form had been drafted by Stephenson & Turner Architects in 1977 when the Council held an exhibition of development proposals for the QVB. Alan Lawrence from Stephenson & Turner further refined the design and in 1980, presented it to Council, though not as a formal tender.

In April 1980, a week before the Council's deadline for lease tenders, a Malaysian businessman, Yap Lim Sen, was in Sydney visiting an Australian business associate, James Barrett. A few hours before leaving for London Yap, who knew nothing of the QVB saga, noticed the signs on the facade announcing the Council's

In the streets the status quo *was* being disturbed.
Builders labourers and their supporters challenged
developers, councils and governments on planning
decisions. Protest focused on social as well as
physical fabric. Premier Askin denounced the
'proletarian planning' but many schemes were
abandoned including the redevelopment of the
Rocks.
Photograph John Fairfax & Sons.

The original steel and sandstone structure of one of the twenty minor domes.
Photograph David Moore.

intention to have the building restored.

From Sydney airport, Yap telephoned Barrett and asked him to investigate the possibility of tendering for the project. Later Barrett recalled, 'I dashed to the Town Hall to get a copy of the restoration brief, the fifty-page document setting out the restoration criteria and everything else the Council required of a developer. Yap phoned back at each stop on his way to London. We were only four days from the deadline and there was only time to give the Council a short statement of interest and tell them a detailed proposal was on the way.'

Consulting Engineer Warner Kuttner had offices in Singapore and Malaysia, and had prior experience with Yap's company. Kuttner's firm was responsible for putting together the consulting group: primarily architects Rice & Daubney for their experience in shopping centres and Stephenson & Turner for their history of involvement with the QVB and their elegant and successful restoration of the Strand Arcade in Sydney. This team formulated the plan Yap's company, Ipoh Garden Berhad, submitted in June 1980.

In one sense Ipoh Garden, a $200 million public company listed on the Kuala Lumpur and Singapore stock exchanges, seemed an unlikely sponsor. Founded in 1964, it had no experience of restoration and no record of major works in Australia. Ipoh Garden was well known in Asia for large and profitable housing, shopping and hotel developments in Malaysia and Hong Kong.

However, Yap and Ipoh Garden's founders, Tan Kim Yeow and Dato Tan Chin Nam (co-owner of the champion racehorse Think Big), were looking for investment and construction opportunities in Australia.

In deciding and deciding quickly to offer to invest in the architectural and commercial revival of the QVB — the first cost estimate was $30 million — they were choosing for their Australian debut an enterprise that was prestigious but also uniquely difficult and something of a gamble. Think Big thus seems a particularly appropriate name for a racehorse owned by a principal investor in the QVB. It is perhaps an omen that the horse won the Melbourne Cup — and not just once, but twice (1974 and 1975).

The first significant Council decision in the long and complex process stretching between proposals and contract came barely three months after the long-awaited 'wealthy visionary' in the form of Yap stepped onto the QVB stage. On 18 August 1980, the Council's QVB panel recommended rejection of the British and Filipino proposals (the Singapore scheme had sunk) because they were, it said 'incompatible' and 'unsatisfactory'. The panel commended the Ipoh Garden proposal to the Council, and advised it to negotiate in detail with the company on its plans to establish a high-quality retail centre in a restored Victorian setting.

Approval of the Ipoh plan also came from the key conservation groups. The Heritage Council described it as a 'highly commendable scheme worthy of further development'. The National Trust urged the Council to accept the Ipoh offer 'without

The Green Bans had dramatic press coverage. Their
significance lay in raising public consciousness about
the state of the cities.
Photograph John Fairfax & Sons.

111

Left: The extraordinary spaces had been cluttered incongruously with boxes of offices; an air-conditioning duct cornered the spiral staircase leading to the centre dome.
Photograph David Moore.

Opposite: And on the roof, impervious to the decades of argument and turmoil, McIntosh's statues look down on another Sydney institution, Gowings...'Walk thru — no one asked to buy'.
Photograph Kraig Carlstrom.

delay' because 'it meets the restoration criteria' and 'is acceptable to the Trust in its philosophy and details'. And Professor Peter Webber, of the Faculty of Architecture at Sydney University said that a majority of the Friends of the QVB approved and that 'the proposal deserves the full support of the authorities'.

For the first time in the long and controversial search for a solution to the QVB dilemma, a plan had emerged on which there was general agreement among Council, conservationists, architects and developers.

The negotiations about plans, leases and finances that the panel had advised continued for almost three years. There was hard bargaining and some political fuss. Sometimes the talks faltered, but they did not fail. Finally, on 1 August 1983 the Lord Mayor, Alderman Doug Sutherland, and Jim Barrett, representing

Ipoh Garden, signed the agreement for restoration of the building and a ninety-nine year profit-sharing lease.

Ninety years before, excavations for the building had begun. Twenty-four years before, Alderman Jensen had suggested demolishing it. Twelve years before, Alderman McDermott had announced its preservation. And it would be a little over three years before restoration would be complete.

At the signing ceremony held in the QVB Lord Mayor Sutherland had a special guest, Mr Malcolm McRae, son of George McRae, architect of the QVB. Malcolm McRae, aged eighty-eight, had been born during construction of his father's masterwork. As a child he had seen the great building rising in Victorian Sydney. He had lived to see it emerge from half a century of decline to the promise of restoration to its former splendour.

RESTORED TO GLORY

FOR the long last act of the saga of the saving of the QVB, the building itself became the stage. A cast of hundreds — architects, engineers, technicians and skilled trade and craft workers — descended upon the derelict. The descriptions of what they were doing ranged from the breathless to the irreverent to the technical. One gushing publicist wrote of 'the Renaissance of Sydney's Sleeping Beauty' and compared the hectic activity on George Street to the kiss of the handsome prince who awoke the legendary princess, a comparison which might or might not have amused the elderly widowed Queen Victoria. A tabloid newspaper announced, 'An old girl's facelift begins to take the Grande Dame of Sydney back to her original grandeur.'

Among some architects there was debate about a more precise and dignified description than 'kiss' or 'facelift'. Words such as 'renewal', 'recycling', 'revitalisation' and 'refurbishment' were used in professional papers. But the owner, the Sydney City Council, the developer, Ipoh Garden Berhad and leading conservationists (including the eminent environment writer of the *Herald*, Joseph Glascott) all defined the great enterprise as 'restoration', a word broad and bold enough to cover a complex process. Indeed, the Council's principal document of direction to developers was entitled the 'Restoration Brief'. It was not quite a tablet of graven stone but it was a weighty sermon which the restorers came to know by heart in the five years it took them to convert it to reality. Dog-eared copies of 'the brief' were *de rigueur* on the drafting boards and desks in the makeshift offices the designers and contractors set up in the QVB.

Among the first things the temporary tenants had to do was to clear the cluttered decks for action, to empty the interior to recover the original space. To knock the old place back into shape they had, literally, to knock a lot of things down. They were all eminently expendable.

There was a happy orgy of demolition, a sort of reverse vandalism as layers and decades of ugly and incongruous additions and alterations were swept aside. Like miners shifting overburden to get at precious metals but with the care of archaeologists lifting modern debris in search of early treasure, the restorers gradually got back to the building's past as they prepared for its future.

They cut away the plywood of the 1960s, the fibro of the 1950s, the concrete of the 1940s, the art deco panels of the 1930s and other partitions and patinas of indeterminate vintages. Slowly the restorers revealed a spectacle they had never seen but that they instantly recognised from sepia-tinted photographs taken at the turn of the century. It was the architectural equivalent of a descent to the long-lost saloons of the *Titanic* — or the revelation of the outlines of an Old Master hidden beneath layers of inferior paintings on some battered canvas.

In this case the canvas was vast — several hectares of space, structure, and surfaces at the disposal of the architects and the marketing experts — with the City Council and the conservationists looking over their shoulders.

Each group had separate but convergent interests. The Ipoh

114

Hiding her face in shame, the grand old building had
to suffer indignities such as newspaper headlines
'VICKI'S PLACE!' and 'Drab George St dowager has
her face lifted'.
Photograph Jenny Templin.

The main dome and cupola required extensive
rebuilding and resurfacing. The interior
atmospherics remained intact.

Photographs Kraig Carlstrom.

The ground floor resembling any underground carpark with only the remains of the art deco lights hinting at what had been in the decades since the 30s. Of the original interior there remain only a bunch of abused arches.

Photograph Jenny Blain.

company wanted the building to include modern elements to make it work efficiently, while retaining historic form and atmosphere to make it distinctive in a highly competitive retail market where style and ambience are as persuasive as rents and prices.

The architects had to consider their clients who employed them, their peers who would judge them and the restoration brief which could censor them.

The Council, led by Mayor Doug Sutherland, had to ensure a financial future for the building — otherwise it would face decay and demolition — and at the same time insist on a restoration standard satisfactory to a generation of citizens who had fought for preservation.

The conservationists, led by the Heritage Council and the National Trust, sought a restoration sensitive to history, but they recognised that a museum approach could, literally, win only a hollow victory. The QVB would be empty.

Thus all the vested interests had considerable common ground. There was also the less tangible but potent influence of prestige. In corporate and community terms, none could contemplate the public relations disaster of failure through insoluble dispute. A collapse of the QVB project would have had all the makings of an architectural and political controversy comparable to the furore over the construction of the Sydney Opera House. There was proof, too, that Sydney's capacity for argument about its cityscape and urban environment was far from exhausted. Even while the QVB was being restored a bitter fight

erupted in 1985 over the proposed construction of a monorail across the city. The debate, the loudest since the era of the 'green bans', pitted the New South Wales government and the monorail company TNT against the City Council, the state opposition, the conservationists, a section of the union movement and the architectural and town planning professions. As the QVB reopened, the monorail dispute was still raging and likely to continue to do so for some time. Thus a long list of factors powerfully concentrated the minds of all concerned with the QVB on ways to avoid controversy and achieve tolerable compromises between historic preservation and commercial enterprise.

Although the architects had fat files of old plans and photographs to guide the 2500 drawings they made for the restoration of the interiors, there was one unknown: what colours had they been? The shapes were clear, but what were the shades? This was a major mystery which posed practical and aesthetic dilemmas. The Ipoh company's retailing experts naturally wanted something memorable, a colour scheme which would impress their tenants and customers. The architects had an eye to history first. The answer was sought somewhere between the letter and spirit of the building. The solution may be contentious and is certainly spectacular; rarely has colour been integrated more prominently into a major commercial centre. And both admirers and critics of the colour schemes had to recognise that there are no true texts against which to test their opinions. The choices remained matters of taste.

The top floor illustrates graphically how almost
nothing of the original interior remained.

Photograph Jenny Blain.

Above: The roof with corrugated iron still in place and work commencing on the main dome.
Opposite: Stripping out of the decades of remodelling begin to expose the marvellous centre void.

Photographs Kraig Carlstrom.

With many decades of inappropriate additions stripped away, restoration begins among a forest of scaffolding.

Photographs Kraig Carlstrom.

Although it was known that the interiors had been extremely decorative in plasterwork, tiling, glass, wrought iron and other architectural detailing, the City Council Archives did not record colour schemes or paints. The photographs, taken long before colour film, suggested a monochromatic colour scheme. Scrapings of plaster and paint more than eighty years old from the newly exposed walls yielded only flakes of green and buff. The steel roof trusses retained their green paint and fragments of tiles and stained glass gave other clues.

The architects commissioned designer Desmond Freeman to assist in devising a credible colour scheme and theme historically accurate within the recorded paint range of the late Victorian period and the colour usage in other Victorian-era buildings in Australia which were better preserved or documented.

The solution had to be comprehensive, and had also to compliment the proportions — the long sunlit upper galleries, for instance, required brighter tones than the smaller, curving surfaces. The result, rich and varied, was not claimed as authentic reproduction, because the original is not known. But the blues, greens, terra-cotta red, pink and mauve which now enliven the QVB are typical of the known nineteenth-century palette, and the colours are faithful to the Victorians' passion for decoration and display. 'The Victorians were not frightened of colour,' Freeman pointed out.

Buried beneath the streets surrounding the QVB island are vital organs of the inner workings of the city of Sydney. In cross-section, the pattern of these concealed components of the civic engine resemble something between a club sandwich and a bowl of spaghetti. There are layers and levels of tubes, pipes, tunnels, ducts, wires — a maze carrying water, electricity, gas, sewage, telephone lines, stormwater, traffic control signals, and the main cross-city railway lines. The QVB teams sliced into this sandwich and probed the pasta-like tangle to excavate pedestrian tunnels and the car park. These are the building's less visible assets but, figuratively and literally, and physically and financially, they are part of its bottom line.

The 720-car car park, at the same level as the ships on Sydney Harbour, is twenty metres deep. It is intended as the financial foundation of the QVB revival, a solid source in solid rock of revenues to supplement rents from retailers and restaurants. In one sense the ornate arcades and galleries of boutiques and bistros are the economic icing, on top of the car park as the seven-layer cake.

Constructing the car park required ingenious engineering gymnastics. The Council and adjacent businesses insisted that one lane of York Street be kept open to traffic during the excavations. So a temporary roadway, supported by concrete piers braced by rock anchors, was cantilevered over the huge hole, providing a bridge for cars and trucks above the drilling and digging.

More engineering contortions were needed to shoehorn some 300 metres of pedestrian and shopping arcades under the building and below George, Market and Druitt streets. These

**The completed inner glass dome resembling an
enormous tiffany lampshade.**

Photograph Jenny Templin.

York Street turned temporarily into a canyon for the car park excavation, with the QVB perched nervously at its edge.

Photograph Jenny Templin.

Manequins in undress-rehearsal in the gallery shopfronts.
Photograph Jenny Templin.

tunnels, lined with shops and cafes, link the QVB to Town Hall railway station and to Grace Bros department store. This ended the long commercial isolation of the QVB's island site by connecting it to Sydney's spreading network of underground arcades, the 'second city' which emerged or submerged in the 1980s under the footpaths between the Town Hall and Martin Place.

The restored QVB belies the magnitude and complexity of the task undertaken by the architects and contractors, as virtually nothing of the original interior remained. From old photographs, from some of McRae's drawings and from contemporary newspaper accounts, the QVB has been restored into a commercially viable retailing complex, notwithstanding the differing interests of the developer, the National Trust and the Heritage Council. As well, a balance was found between the interests of fire protection and safety, and the maintenance of the essential architectural character.

The architects were faced with a continual process of negotiation and problem solving, bringing their creative abilities to the handling and resolving of the conflicting issues, to retain architectural integrity while introducing modern technology and current retailing requirements. The completed building is evidence that this goal was achieved by remarkable perserverance and with singular success.

Restored to glory.
Photograph Jenny Templin.

THE LADY HAS A FUTURE

THE QVB reopened in the last days of 1986, a splendid Christmas present for Sydney, a glittering gift to the city. Like all good things, it was well worth waiting for. It arrived with a bang in the form of the popping of celebratory champagne corks and a blaze of publicity praising its space and grace, its beauty and its pleasures. Suddenly, the initials 'QVB' passed into the language of the city, a shorthand expression evoking both a slice of history and a new marvel of commerce.

The domes, distinctive as any trademark, were officially depicted on motor-vehicle registration stickers and on the cover of the Sydney telephone book. Indeed, the Lord Mayor, Alderman Sutherland, said he was confident that the QVB would attain the same visual status as a symbol of Sydney as the Harbour Bridge and the Opera House. The *Herald* commented, 'It has taken Sydney almost ninety years to appreciate the Queen Victoria Building' — and Sydney seemed intent on making up for lost time.

In the pre-Christmas opening period, fifty thousand shoppers and visitors flocked to the building each day. At the QVB, happy days were there again. And, as exuberant as the bubbles in the opening toasts, there was a surge of civic pride. The Lord Mayor declared that it was 'the most spectacular retailing area in Australia'. It was also an instant favourite with tourists and a joy to fashion photographers.

If the shade of the original architect George McRae mingled with the shoppers, he could certainly recognise the born-again QVB. All his classic Victorian forms and fancies are in place — arches, curved staircases, plaster motifs, columns, wrought iron balustrades, colourful tiles, stained glass, lofty atriums, barrel vault glass roof and so on.

The combination of the old elegance and the modern retailing elements mark the marriage of ostensibly divergent interests — history and commerce. And it was an instructive example for planners elsewhere in an increasingly significant field of international architecture: the restoration of heritage buildings.

When the QVB reopened in time for Christmas shopping, there were memories and ghosts galore to recall at the celebrations. There was, also, a new list of names to honour in the archives. Alderman Sutherland and the Sydney City Council had been a main moving force in the enterprise. Ipoh Garden Berhad, and in particular Yap Lim Sen and James Barrett, had through their financial courage caused the enterprise to become a reality. In addition, the principal architects Ross Gardner, John Daubney, Alan Lawrence and George Kringas of the joint venture architects Rice & Daubney, Stephenson & Turner led the consulting team which, together with the principal contractors A.W. Edwards and K.B. Hutchenson and other members of the construction industry, brought the enterprise to a successful conclusion.

For all concerned, the restoration had involved risks. The Queen Victoria Building had long known difficult times and no guarantees of success could be given at its reopening. However, the prospects were good. And its history suggested that somehow there was built into the stone an asset even stronger than style: a spirit of survival.

Photograph David Moore.

Long a dark and silent building, life returns to the QVB at night.
Photograph David Moore.

The marvellous restored tiling of The Avenue.
Photograph Christopher Shain.

The centre dome again is the principal focus of
the interior.

Photograph David Moore.

Above: The grand staircase on York Street which was totally reconstructed.
Photograph David Moore.

Opposite: The dominance of the dome viewed from York Street.
Photograph David Moore.

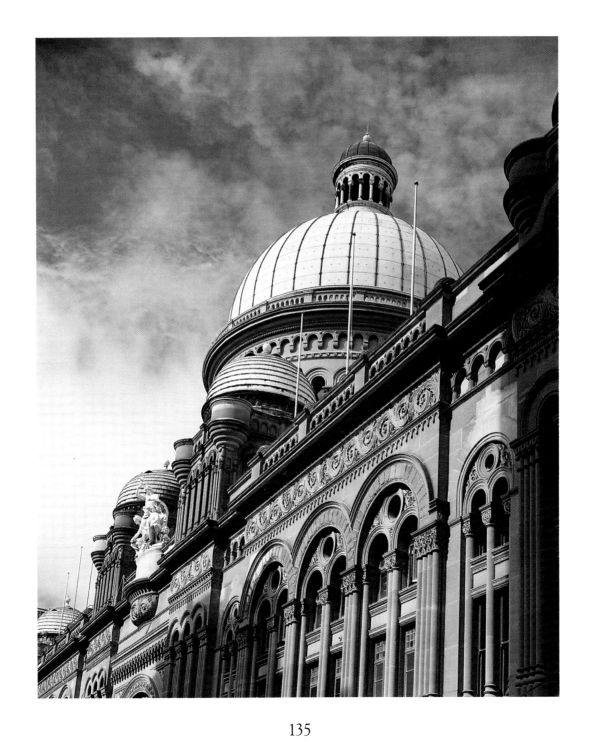

Above: The restored galleries with the dome visible through the glass roof.

Photograph David Moore.

Opposite: The main dome, spectacularly floodlit at night is even more dramatic against the backdrop of starkly modern offices.

Photograph David Moore.

The view into the gallery from a shop on the first
floor. The leadlight windows were reproduced from
original details.
Photograph David Moore.

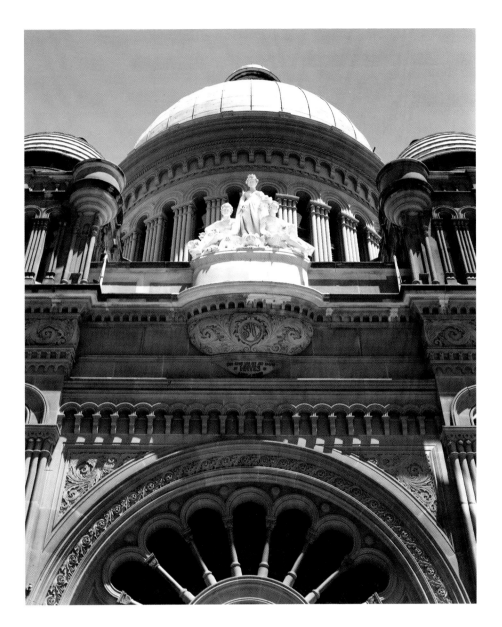

McIntosh's statues gaze in a proprietorial fashion
from the resurrected QVB.

Photograph David Moore.

The original spiral staircase, once again in congenial surroundings.

Photograph David Moore.

A detail from the elaborate interior shows the elegant colour scheme.

Photograph David Moore.

A view over the glazed barrel vault roof.

Photograph David Moore.

The main George Street leadlight
window — the missing centre panel was
redesigned to commemorate the
building and its restoration in 1986.
Photograph David Moore.

An enthusiastic welcome as a grand public space is
returned to the city of Sydney.

Photograph Jenny Templin.